ROOSTER TALES

This 1968 photo of the author was taken at a regatta
in northern Oklahoma. This Class-D runabout is a
Desilva powered by a modified Mark 55H Mercury.

MEMORIES OF A
BOAT RACER

DUDLEY MALONE

authorHOUSE®

AuthorHouse™
1663 Liberty Drive
Bloomington, IN 47403
www.authorhouse.com
Phone: 1 (800) 839-8640

Published by AuthorHouse 02/01/2018

ISBN: 978-1-5462-2546-1 (sc)
ISBN: 978-1-5462-2545-4 (e)

Library of Congress Control Number: 2018900878

Print information available on the last page.

CONTENTS

PROLOGUE

The war was over. It was a hot, windy Independence Day on Lake Texoma on the Red River between Oklahoma and Texas, and it was the first big boat race held in the Southwest since before the attack on Pearl Harbor.

Drivers from Oklahoma, Texas, and surrounding states—many of whom had just returned from Europe, Italy, and the South Pacific—were ready to take up where they had been interrupted nearly five years earlier. There was also several thousand dollars in prize money at stake.

I don't recall any of the winners that day, other than Texan G. G. Slack of Dallas, Texas, a well-known figure in racing at that time. I remember him because of the county sheriff incident that afternoon in which Slack and my father, the race chairman, got into a rhubarb over the prize money Slack had won. The lawman's presence cooled the argument, and Slack went on to become one of my favorites in the racing fraternity over the years. He also went on to win a national championship several years later.

As the Texoma regatta was a professional race, most of the boats were hydroplanes—some conventional single-step designs and others the newer three-point style. The boats were plank-bottom hulls, mostly mahogany, and were built by Willis, Jacoby, Flowers, Century, and other familiar names of the time.

Because Texoma was choppy that day, I remember the single-step hulls fared better than the three-pointers.

Competition that Thursday afternoon sported boats in A, B, C, C Service, and F classes. All engines in the races, except for the A Class, were laterally opposed cylinder designs primarily by Johnson and Evinrude, which had ruled the racing roost before the United States entered World War II in 1941. The smaller A engines were mostly two-cylinder inline KR model Johnsons.

With most of the drivers being veteran racers and recently discharged US veterans, they were eager to get back on the water. Some hadn't fired an engine since the late summer of 1941. The Texoma race was disappointing for many, however, as they spent the entire day cranking and swearing at the stubborn, balky, methanol-fueled outboards. In some cases, the engines contained less alcohol than their owners, as I recall.

I don't remember many other details of that day, but I had a great time. In fact, I caught a fever that Fourth of July that has lasted more than seventy years!

POSTWAR ERA

1945–1949

After the United States declared victory in Europe and the South Pacific, hundreds of thousands of young men returned home, many still craving the newfound excitement they had experienced from international travel and, in many cases, combat.

It was natural that those who had raced outboards before the war would want to get back on the water. The resurgence of boat racing during the late 1940s was evidence of pent-up demand created by four years of national austerity and personal sacrifice.

In the professional ranks, most of the competitors were prewar jockeys who had retrieved their plank-hull hydroplanes and runabouts from mothballs. Their engines were prewar cast-iron block mills, primarily the Evinrude Midget (M class), the Johnson KR (A class), SR (B class), and PR (C class). The Evinrude and Elto 4-60s, Evinrude Big Four, and Pumpers dominated the big F class, while the Evinrude Speeditwin, Johnson P-50, and PO models raced in the very competitive C Service class.

Most engines had been designed and built in the 1930s, and as parts became scarce, the need for new supplies became acute. As a result, numerous aftermarket parts manufacturers

1

and fabricators emerged. These included Oklahoman Frank Vincent, a multinational champion during the 1930s, Clyde Wiseman, originator of Wiseco Pistons, which are used today in all types of engines, Henry Fuller, Wes Jones, and others. Probably the largest parts maker of the time, however, was Pep Hubbell, an enterprising innovator in El Monte, California. Pep built almost everything for the old "alky" motors of the day and even assembled complete engines for sale. By the end of the decade, most of the old alky burners contained very few parts built by their original manufacturers.

During the 1940s, the boat designs changed little from their prewar brethren. They had slightly more streamlined appearances but were very heavy by today's featherweight standards. The leading shingles bore names such as Jacoby, Neal, and Fillinger, while the front-running runabouts were built by Desilva, Willis, and others.

Alky burners are shown negotiating a turn in a southern Texas race in the late '40s. All three of these B class boats are powered by Johnson SR engines. The front rig (T-23) is a conventional (or single-step) hydro, which is followed closely by a three-pointer. During the '40s, both conventional and three-point hydros were popular, and several drivers would carry both types and choose which to use after viewing water conditions at the race site. The conventional was generally the choice if the water was rough. (Photo origin unknown.)

Professional outboard drivers of the postwar era were cast as greasy, cigar-smoking, macho guys who duked it out with fists and wrenches after the races and between beers. There were some just like that, but many others, such as Bill Tenny or Frank Vincent, did not fit that mold. Most of the competitors of the day would do about anything to win a race, but when a fellow driver needed something, he could count on almost anyone in the pits to help out. In most cases, the old driver of the 1940s was a lot harder on the exterior than the interior. As most of them were veterans who had survived the "big war," it was difficult for some to make the transition from military to civilian life. Some even used outboard racing as an outlet for frustrations born of the war.

During that period, Americans had money in their pockets for the first time since the Great Depression, television had not yet made the scene, and people were longing for recreation. Attending sporting events became an obsession that greatly boosted outboard racing, as well as other summer sports such as baseball and auto racing. As a result of this popularity, speedboat races sprang up on almost every body of water large enough to accommodate a course. Some of these events were sanctioned by the American Power Boat Association and attended by well-known pilots of the day. However, probably most regattas were unsanctioned outlaw events in which you could spot a variety of factory and homemade hulls powered by stock and modified service engines.

During the postwar period, the sport received a shot in the arm when, in 1947, Carl Keikhaefer, a brilliant German outboard manufacturer, introduced his Mercury model KE7 Lightning Deluxe engine. Rated as 10 horsepower, this powerful little package was 19.8 cubic inches and weighed only 59 pounds, considerably less than its competition of that day. This power plant grew in popularity among racers until 1949, when Mercury introduced its Model KF7 Super Ten. Though the same size as the KE7, it was a little faster and, therefore, became the dominant B-class stock engine. Also in 1949, Mr. Keikhaefer really did himself proud when Mercury rolled out a new 25-horsepower model called a Thunderbolt Model KF9.

With a bore and stroke identical to the two-cylinder KE7 and KF7 models, this inline four-cylinder mill weighed only 122 pounds and had a 39.6-cubic-inch displacement. This machine revived the old D class, which had a maximum of forty cubic inches and had become almost extinct. The following year, Mercury introduced the KG-7, which held most B-class titles for the next four years.

I'll never forget my first view of the four-cylinder Thunderbolt in action. It happened at the annual July 4 regatta in Catfish Bay on Lake Texoma in 1949. The day's events had gone as expected, with the usual opposed-cylinder "big-iron" rigs fighting it out in the larger classes. The last and most exciting event of the day was the Free for All race that any outboard could enter. A large field of 33- and 50-horsepower jobs was on hand, each expecting to take home the coveted FFA trophy. When the five-minute gun sounded, about ten of the big rigs (all runabouts) were fired off, and the entire bank shook with their throaty roar.

About a minute later, after most of the big-iron boats had planed off and were preparing to start the heat, we heard the strange, high-pitched whine of a white runabout parked at the far end of the course and not started prior to this event. The excitement generated by this strange sound made everyone run to the shoreline to witness what was about to happen. The white runabout with its strange green engine was driven by a pilot named Tex Flagg, who lived just forty miles away in the north Texas town of Sherman. The rig was owned by Bill Bell, one of Mercury Marine's first distributors.

The white boat with the weird inline four-cylinder engine did not win the Free for All race that day; a 33-horsepower job did. But Tex did place second behind one of the hottest boats in the Southwest, and he sure woke up a bunch of people. Tex was a great driver, and he won the APBA Class D Stock National Championship the following year in Dallas, Texas, in that same white boat. Bill Bell also fielded an A-class runabout driven by Al Montouri, who also won a national championship in the 1950 Dallas races.

In 1949, two other motor manufacturers, Martin and Champion, joined Mercury in producing high-speed engines designed for stock racing. The National Pressure Cooker Company had earlier manufactured a powerful little outboard designated the Martin 60. Due to its success and the rising popularity of outboard racing, the manufacturer decided to enter the competition market with a new product it called the Martin Hi-Speed 60. The stock version of this power plant was rated at 7.2 horsepower. However, the new racing version, designed by professional driver George Martin, was said to have developed 16 horsepower on a dynamometer at 6,000 rpm. This engine was never formally accepted by the American Power Boat Association because of its size: eleven cubic inches. However, numerous other clubs and organizations did accept the engine, and it was raced into the early 1950s.

Champion's 1949 racing debut featured a potent little 12.4-cubic-inch power plant called the Hot Rod Special. This engine, a modified version of Champion's 7.9-horsepower fishing motor, was the Minneapolis-based company's first model that would impact the racing community for the next several years.

A well-known racing team of the '40s and '50s was the Morphys' Shooting Star Racing Team. Lewis Morphy was a top C-class contender in the alky ranks. His wife, Boots, drove one of the best midget hydros in the country. Lewis was a well-known Hollywood stunt actor, and Boots was a popular stunt actress. (Photo origin unknown.)

During the postwar years up to 1949, the American Power Boat Association had two divisions of outboard racing: Division I for amateurs and Division II for the professionals. Championships were conducted separately for each division, though usually at the same regatta. Most of the well-known names in outboard racing at that time were Division II drivers. Many of these, such as Paul Wearly, Bud Wiget, Don Whitfield, Don Frazier, and Bill Tenny, had competed during the prewar era. However, many new faces began appearing in the postwar 1940s and made their presence known in the winner's circle.

In 1946, the first outboard championships after World War II were held on the West Coast, at Long Beach, the Salton Sea in California, and Lake Mead in Nevada. All the champions that year resided on the West Coast with two drivers—Ed Silva in Division I and Norris Dutcher in Division II—winning double championships.

In 1947, the C Service Hydroplane and F Racing Runabout class championships were held again at the Salton Sea, an area where many participants in those classes were located. Championships for the balance of the classes were held in Brownwood, Texas, a hotbed of activity in the Lone Star State. There, Paul Wearly gained acclaim by winning the very competitive B and C classes in the Professional Division.

Celina, Tennessee, a sleepy town near the Kentucky border, was the scene of the 1948 National Championships. There Paul Wearly (Class C-II) and Don Frazier (Class F-I) repeated championship performances of the previous year. Two drivers at the Tennessee race won dual championships: Ted Benda in Division I C Service Runabout and C Racing Runabout and Clyde Wiseman (of Wiseco Piston fame) in Division II C Service Runabout and C Racing Runabout.

In 1949, the largest national championship regatta since the war was staged on Lake Alfred, Florida in late September. A large entry list was present from the alky ranks, but what made this event special was the introduction of the stock utilities at a national championship. The first few days of the event were devoted to the "alky burners," with all the familiar "big guns" of the time present. Winners in the alky hydro brackets that year included Don Whitfield (Class M), Mabry Edwards (Class A), Paul Wearly (Class B), Doug Creech (Class C), Bud Wiget (C Service), and Orville Lowe (F Class). The Runabout-only classes were topped by Jack Stanford (C Racing) and Rich Gebhardt (C Service). The popular Free for All event was captured by Marshall Eldredge of nearby Lakeland, Florida, in a boat propelled by a very potent Draper X engine, a specially designed mill by the well-known hop-up artist Dean Draper.

The stock-utility portion of the big six-day program wound up the show. Termed very successful by the entire racing fraternity, this new division of racing featured numerous new drivers, engines, and boats. The idea behind this new racing concept was to provide a niche for competitors with restricted purses or a lack of engine savvy, to compete on an even level with their competition. Existing alky classes at that time were comprised of special built-for-racing engines that were temperamental and expensive, and specially designed for racing hulls that only accommodated the driver. The new category of racing limited engines to strictly stock mills, which had to run on gasoline. The boats were two-cockpit hulls designed to permit a passenger or passengers to ride in the front. Such a rig could be used to take the family for a Sunday ride at the local lake or compete in one of the many regattas held each weekend in just about any section of the country. This was a great concept, which was fueled primarily by Keikhaefer Marine, whose engines powered the majority of hulls used during the early days of this division.

The first Stock Utility National champions and the records they set at the Lake Alfred Regatta were:

Class	Driver	Address	Record (MPH)
JU	Roy Ridgell	Gainesville, FL.	20.689
AU	Paul Wearly	Muncie, IN	28.758
BU	Jon Culver	Dayton, OH	34.201
CU	Charles Wingo	Baltimore, MD	33.088
DU	Jack Maypole	Chicago, IL	38.994

During the 1940s, my personal involvement with racing was as a spectator and a wannabe racer. I obtained my first boat in 1949, a second or third-hand Penn Yan hull on which we mounted what I thought at the time was a powerful 12-horsepower Sea-Bee outboard my dad had purchased from the Goodyear Tire and Rubber Company. My father had been a Goodyear tire dealer for a number of years, and he had ordered a small stock of these Gale Products–built motors for resale.

We lived a short distance from Lake Texoma, a huge body of water that borders Oklahoma on its north side and Texas on its south. Dad had, I believe, purchased the second boat ever launched on this lake. It was a real beauty, a Gar Wood three-cockpit inboard runabout that had been built sometime during the 1930s. It was powered by a gigantic Hispano Suiza World War I fighter-plane engine which provided a fast ride when it ran. Unfortunately, it required about ten hours of mechanical work for every hour of running time. Dad did all the wrenching on it, so he became very proficient with that machine. The "Hisso" engine, as it was termed, had gained considerable fame in the 1920s and 1930s for its use in racing cars of that era. The Gar Wood was purchased during World War II and was used by our family every summer until my father was fatally injured in a car wreck in 1961.

During the early postwar years, the popularity of boating in general was on the rise. A favorite pastime of many of the local citizens of our hometown was to take a Sunday afternoon drive out to the lake to watch the boats. Consequently, my dad spent many an afternoon giving the local citizenry rides in the "ole Hisso." Of course, I usually tagged along and generally took my seat in the rear cockpit so I could feel the boat's spray.

We had a lot of great memories in the Gar Wood, one of which occurred on a Sunday afternoon just after the war's end. The US Navy was in town doing some promotion activity and was demonstrating one of its landing crafts in the same area Dad's boat was kept. When the landing craft left the dock, two sailors dressed in their white uniforms were operating the craft with a score of locals aboard. The navy personnel explained that the boat was safe and could not get stuck, even on the muddy bank of Lake Texoma. After all, this type of craft had transported thousands to the beaches at Normandy, Anzio, and countless islands in the South Pacific. About an hour after the landing craft left, it was sighted about a mile down the lake, of all things, stuck in the mud. Dad pulled up alongside in the Gar Wood and asked the navy boys if they needed any help. They just laughed, said the landing craft weighed X number of tons, and that the little twenty-three-footer wouldn't be any help.

We then continued our ride and drove back by the stuck craft an hour later. At that point, the "swabbies" were at their wits' end, having tried everything they knew to free it. They were very embarrassed, and everyone on board was hot, thirsty, and losing patience. This time they agreed to a tow rope from the Gar Wood, though they exclaimed they didn't see how it would help. Dad then cranked up the ole Hisso and, to the astonishment of all concerned, pulled the landing craft out to clear water before the sailors could even start the engines in the landing craft. We all got a big kick out of this, and the feat became the talk of the town the following week.

THE GOLDEN YEARS

1950–1959

The 1950s have often been termed the "golden years," a fitting tribute for outboard racing. The emphasis placed on racing in the late forties by Mercury was carried into the fifties, to the extent that the word *Mercury* became almost synonymous with outboard racing. Other engines competing in stock racing during that period were the Martin Hi-Speed 60 and Silver Streak 200 models, the Champion Hot Rods, the Evinrude & Johnson 22-horsepower motors, and a few Chris Craft and Scott Atwaters. During the early part of the decade, the Evinrude 33-horsepower model was also used in the "E" class, though this motor was phased out by the mid-1950s. Another Outboard Marine Corp. (OMC) product, a 25-horsepower model, saw limited competition in a class designated as "D-1," but this class did not make much impact on the racing scene.

By the mid-1950s, the Champion Hot Rod was Mercury's only competition in the popular "A" and "B" classes, and this was in limited numbers. Beginning with the models KG4 (A Class), KG7 (B Class), and KG9 (D Class), which Mercury introduced in 1950, these engines were upgraded and replaced by faster models during the decade. In 1954, the Mark 20H was introduced to replace the KG7H. This was probably the most famous but controversial outboard racing engine ever produced by the Keikhaefer Corporation. The reason for its controversy was its threat to completely make obsolete the old KG7H engine, which had gained so much in popularity during its four-year supremacy of the B Class. As a solution to this dilemma, Keikhaefer introduced a conversion kit to change the twenty-cubic-inch KG7 power head to a fifteen-cubic-inch KG4 Class A engine for the price of only $72.87. This conversion was a major reason for the popularity and competition enjoyed in the A Class during the 1950s.

Mercury also updated its engines used in other racing classes during the decade. In 1953, it produced the Mark 40H Class D motor, which made the KG9H obsolete. In 1956, that engine was replaced by the Mark 55H, a die-cast forty-cubic-inch inline Class D job that really rewrote the record books. Mercury entered the Class C market in 1956 with its Mark 30H model and even produced a limited number of sixty-cubic-inch six-cylinder inline Class F engines, termed Mark 75H, in the mid-1950s.

Meanwhile, Evinrude and Johnson, who had not actively pursued the racing market since the 1930s, were also unintentionally still involved in racing activity with their two-cylinder Big Twin and 30-horsepower models utilized in the "Stock 36" and D-1 classes. Until Mercury's Mark 30H model was introduced, the opposed-cylinder Evinrude and Johnsons were also dominant in the C Class. In addition, the Evinrude opposed four-cylinder 33-horsepower model was used in the E Class, though these mills were phased out in the mid-1950s.

Jud Davis was a tough competitor in the Missouri and Illinois areas in the early '50s. Here he is shown in his Class F Neal runabout "Chubby." Unlike most modern outboard racing hulls, which bear no identity marks except racing numbers, boats of the postwar era and '50s bore names, which helped spectators identify them. Dick Neal's boat company was best known for the hydroplanes it built. However, the Neal runabout was also a very competitive hull. (Photo origin unknown)

In the professional or alky ranks, the engines used during the early part of the decade remained unchanged from those of the postwar era, with the cast-iron block jobs being used almost exclusively. The replacement parts difficulties experienced by racers of the 1940s were eased by a number of specialty houses such as Hubbell, Henry Fuller, and Wiseco, which produced parts for these engines.

In the mid and late 1950s, however, the modified Mercurys and even some Champions began challenging the old engines. The obsolescence of the old motors became a reality in the late 1950s, when Quincy Welding Company and Pep Hubbell developed and produced tuned exhaust systems. Other modifications to the Mercs by these two engine hop-up specialists and others, such as Dick O'Dea in New Jersey, provided much-improved high-speed performance.

During the early years of stock-engine modifications, the professional divisions resisted entry into their ranks by the modified stockers. In order to accommodate these engines, a separate division, termed Division IV, was created by the National Outboard Association. This became a very successful segment that was eventually melted into the Professional Division (or Division I) of the NOA in 1958. The reason for its acceptance into the professional ranks at that time was not to accommodate the modified boys but to bolster the ranks of the professional classes, which had become almost extinct.

Racing-boat designs and construction changed dramatically in the 1950s. Most of the boat builders of the 1940s continued production into the next decade. These included Jacoby, Neal, Fillinger, Willis, Speedliner, and a host of others. Boats in the 1940s had been generally plank-bottom hulls designed for the heavy cast-iron engines. To accommodate the rising popularity of the lighter aluminum-stock racing engines being produced in the 1950s, a number of new boats with unfamiliar names began to surface. Some of these included Sid Craft, Swift, Rinker, and Pabst, which began taking the limelight. The newer hulls featured much lighter construction, with all-plywood exteriors and aerodynamic designs that enabled them to lift and handle much better than the earlier designs.

Runabouts began being built with lower profiles for better wind resistance, and their lighter plywood skins which made them considerably faster. The hydroplane, on the other hand, received a boost with lighter construction techniques, but aerodynamics and the use of air traps on their bottoms really enhanced the speed and performance of these craft. In the early 1950s, I can remember that the popular thought among drivers was that smaller is better. It was common to see eight-foot Class A (15-cubic-inch) and Class B (20-cubic-inch) hydros or ten-foot Class D (40-cubic-inch) hydroplanes, unthinkable lengths by today's standards.

This 1953 photo was taken in the pits at the Winnebago Marathon in Wisconsin. Shown here are four all-aluminum hulls built by the Blue Star Boat Company of Miami, Oklahoma. The two A/B runabouts in the foreground were owned and transported to the event by a Kansas Blue Star dealer. The hydroplane and runabout on the trailer were owned and driven by John Jordan, a Kansas wheat farmer. Jordan was very competitive in these boats but suffered bad luck at this marathon race. However, he remained in Wisconsin after the event and raced at Oshkosh the following week, where he scored wins in both the A and B hydroplane classes. These aluminum boats were much lighter in weight than their wooden counterparts, which gave them a definite speed advantage. The trim on them was adjusted by the use of wedges between the framework and the bottom skin. (Photo origin unknown)

A majority of racing boats of the 1940s and early 1950s were transported on individual trailers and the boats unloaded by backing them into the water. This practice was necessary because of the weight of the rigs. They were often towed with their motors mounted on the transoms. Usually, however, the owner removed the lower unit to prevent damage to it while in tow. This was a simple matter, as the unit was taken off by the removal of only two nuts. This also afforded protection for the propeller which, in some cases, was the only propeller, or "wheel" the owner possessed. I can remember numerous other methods also used in the transportation of race boats. These included car-top carriers, in the beds of pickups, and just about any other way imaginable. One such arrangement that comes to mind was orchestrated by Ben Turpin, a wily old veteran of many racing wars who car-topped with his new Cadillac. Most of those who car-topped used their trunks to carry their engine and equipment. Not so with Ben; he pulled out his back seat and gutted the back end, where he installed a motor rack and hauled an engine or two, plus a couple of cans of Chris-Go racing fuel, tools, props, and whatever else was needed to campaign his "B" rig. Ben, curiously, was very partial to Chris-Go, as he appeared on numerous advertisements for that product which appeared in various magazines.

By the mid-1950s, the standard tow became a trailer with a bunk or bunks on its front to accommodate the owner's boat(s) and a motor box on the rear to house the engine(s), propellers, fuel, tools, and whatever else the driver required (and this didn't always include racing equipment). I remember one race I attended fairly close to home, where a couple of acquaintances came over to my pit area to visit. One of them announced that he had always been curious about the contents of the motor boxes on the race-boat trailers, so he had peered into one of them a few trailers down from mine. He said it contained only several cases of beer and a cooler. He said it was so full of the beverage that the driver was having to carry his engine and tools in his automobile trunk. Fortunately, this case was the exception and not the rule, as most of the trailer boxes did contain the multitude of equipment required to get the driver's boat through a race.

Start of the first race of the 1953 season in north Texas. A healthy field of Class B runabouts crosses the line in April on Lake Worth. Thirteen entries are pictured here, but it was commonplace to witness a full field of sixteen entries at races held in that area. (R.E. Thompson photo)

By 1950, the Durant (Oklahoma) Boat Club had moved to Catfish Bay on the west side of Lake Texoma. This was a great spot for boating, and the sport of boat racing flourished there too. Interested members of the boat club formed the Texoma Racing Association, which promoted and conducted an annual regional regatta on the Fourth of July each year, in addition to club races and impromptu races just about every Sunday afternoon during summer months.

The leader of this group was a local tire and Mercury outboard dealer by the name of John Doraty, whom we fondly called "the Admiral." John owned a Speedliner two-cockpit runabout powered by a 22-horsepower Johnson (a C Class rig). His son, Robert, who was a Mercury mechanic, raced a Morphew runabout powered by a KF7 Class B Merc. Other members of the group included Roy Woodruff, John's competitor, who raced a Willis two-cockpit Johnson-powered "C" rig; Buddy Woodruff, who drove a Morphew propelled by a 16-horsepower Evinrude; Bob Cordray (a local car dealer), who fielded a beautiful mahogany Doler runabout with a "B" Merc; and his son Robert, who raced a Speedliner hull. Other active members included Guy Morris and his two boys, Jimmy and Rene, Jimmy Lee, "Fuzz" Tyson, J. D. Summit, and a host of others whose names I can't recall.

I'll never forget looking forward all week to Sunday, when we would tear up old Catfish Bay with the engine noise, the spray, and the wonderful aroma of burning castor oil. Sunday evening there would usually be a picnic or a square dance at a pavilion built near the club's headquarters, located on a hill overlooking the bay. These were some of the most enjoyable moments of my life and they played a large part in my longtime participation in racing.

A lot of interesting and exciting experiences occurred in Catfish Bay. One such experience happened one Sunday afternoon, when one of the club members, who had parked his car on top of the hill near the clubhouse, forgot to put the car in gear and use his emergency brake. I was out on the large club boat dock, working on a motor, when I heard someone yell. I looked up just in time to see the unattended car heading down the hill toward the water. It barely avoided the dock and hit the water, settling in about twenty feet of water. I've always used my emergency brake since that afternoon.

My first boat race as a driver, at age fourteen, occurred at one of the Texoma club races in June of 1950. This was an event I'll never forget. The morning before the races, I had driven out to the lake with Robert Cordray, who had planned to enter the races. My parents had stayed in town and were planning to drive out later in the day. After we arrived at the lake, I untied my Penn Yan, powered by the 12-horsepower Sea Bee and, as was my usual fashion, ran it around the bay at full throttle. In the meantime, Robert's Mercury developed engine trouble, and he had to scratch from the race card. In doing so, he asked if I would like to drive his boat that day. I probably made the quickest decision I had ever made: I told him yes, and within ten minutes, we had removed the Sea Bee from the transom of the Penn Yan and set it on Robert's Speedliner. The Sea Bee didn't have a steering bar or carburetor control for the throttle, so I had to steer it with a tiller handle and run it wide open (which is the way I usually ran anyway).

I entered the 16-horsepower race that day, along with three other boats. I'll always remember the thrill of that race, particularly since I had to run full bore—having no throttle control. Buddy Woodruff nearly lapped me, but I did finish second (thanks to one of the other entries conking out and the fourth boat finishing the heat on one cylinder).

After the event, all the racers parked their rigs at the big boat club dock, and the spectators came down to look them over. I was proudly sitting on the dock by my rig (Robert's Speedliner with my Sea Bee engine). I felt pretty good until a cab driver acquaintance from Durant stopped by and noted that my boat was sure a sleek one but the motor wasn't much. I never did like that guy after that!

Shortly after the visit with the cab driver, my parents drove up. As soon as they exited their car, someone told them I had run in the races. I then received some disparaging remarks from my mother, which prompted my quick exit from the dock. This had been a day to remember, even if it had ended on a slightly negative note.

At the annual July 4 racing event that year in Catfish Bay, staged by the Southwest Power Boat Association, I got a look at what would personally become my first real racing craft. It was a big boat, by those days' standards, which was driven in the 16-horsepower class by, of all people, a woman. This was, to me, an unusual occurrence in a sport dominated by so-called "macho men." Her name was Betty Williams, and she scored second in the race, just behind one of the hottest pilots of the day, Hi Drummond. Her boat, a two-cockpit Doler named *If,* which was owned by Olen Scott of nearby Madill, Oklahoma, handled well. It was a sturdy hull on which a pair of side fins was mounted near the rear of the boat. I fell in love with this craft and, not long after the races, purchased it from Olen with borrowed funds. The boat was a beauty, but I soon found out it was too heavy, as Betty's light weight (about sixty pounds less than me) was one of the reasons for its speed. I was also disappointed to find that the reason for the side fins was to keep the boat right side up. (It had a history of flips.)

At that same July 4 race in 1950, one of my heroes, G. G. Slack of Dallas, Texas, showed up with a fierce-looking round-chine, lap-strake hull with an aluminum nose. The boat was aptly named the *Silver Bullet.* Slack was quite a driver, and he put on a great show that day, winning the 22-horsepower event and scoring high in the 33-horsepower and Free for All events. After the races, I looked over this unusual boat and discovered the aluminum nose consisted of a thin sheet of aluminum wrapped around the front of the wooden hull, which, I believe, was a Dunphy. I mentioned this to one of the drivers standing nearby, who explained that Slack had been in an auto wreck a few weeks earlier while towing the boat to a race. The front end was damaged so ol' Slack just dabbed on a lot of glue around the hole and wrapped it with aluminum. He then stood back, looked at his masterpiece, and remarked that it looked like a bullet. Thus, the name *Silver Bullet.* He also mentioned Slack always liked the Lone Ranger (who made silver bullets a buzzword to all kids in the 1950s)

G. G. Slack from Dallas, Texas was always one of my favorites. Slack is pictured here in a two-cockpit Willis Flying Saucer powered by an Evinrude Speeditwin Class C mill. Slack probably won more races than anyone else in the Southwest during his era. He raced several different classes but was considered the "maestro" in a C Runabout. (Photo origin unknown)

Christmas of 1950 was my all-time best Christmas ever. My mother and brother had driven to Arkansas for the holidays, and my dad and I were to follow on Christmas Eve (as Dad had to work until then). Early on Christmas Eve morning, we drove by Dad's auto agency to check on things before leaving. After drinking several cups of coffee and engaging in a few bull sessions, we hopped in the car and turned into the street heading for Arkansas. My dad suddenly spotted "Humpy" Campbell, owner of the business next door. He stopped in the middle of the street, asked me to roll down the window, and then yelled at Humpy, "May the bluebirds of happiness crap in your Christmas pie." We both started laughing, and Dad, still looking at Humpy, started off in low gear. However, we only traveled about ten feet before we came to a sudden halt, as we had plowed into the back end of another car. So much for Christmas wishes!

That Christmas didn't start out too well, but it sure ended on a good note, as I found my all-time best Christmas present in a note in my stocking. It read, "Merry Christmas, you have a new Mercury 7½-horsepower Hurricane in a box at home." Needless to say, I couldn't wait until we arrived home from the holidays to uncrate my first real racing engine. This "greentop" would eventually power four different boats for me during the next four years.

The next summer (1951), I spent numerous enjoyable hours driving the new Merc on *If* in Catfish Bay. By August, I felt I was ready to take on the world, and we decided to enter the Oklahoma Boat Racing Association's final race of the season, to be held on Lake Sahoma, near Tulsa. I certainly wasn't a world beater in that event, but I was proud to finish a respectable fourth in the "A" Utility Class.

The next year was my first full racing season, and I competed in several different events throughout Oklahoma and northern Texas. In my first race of 1952 at Lake Lugert in southwestern Oklahoma, I witnessed an awesome spectacle of boat racing historical significance that I'll never forget. Vester Acutt, a "B" Runabout driver from Oklahoma City, flipped his Speedliner rig no less than seven times, all in the same day! Vester really made a name for himself in that event, not just for the turnovers but also for his tenacity. Vester was a great guy and very colorful. Later that year, in the same boat, he performed another spectacular feat at Oklahoma City when, on the home stretch, he barrel-rolled his rig 360 degrees, landing upright with Vester still in the cockpit. The engine continued running and, unbelievably, Vester only momentarily slowed down. It all happened so fast that everyone who had witnessed the occurrence wasn't sure it really had happened. The announcer, apparently thinking he was seeing things, didn't make mention of it, and none of the other drivers spoke a word about this unusual event. The following weekend, several of us were gathered on a prerace night, doing our customary Saturday night bench racing, when someone announced he was reluctant to even mention it but he could have sworn he saw Vester Acutt do a 360 the previous weekend and never miss a lick. Everyone in earshot began laughing, as they had all seen it but were afraid to say anything, for fear of being branded crazy.

I won my first trophy (for second place) at the second race in

1952 at Hugo, Oklahoma. The award was only as big as a beer can, but I've never been as proud of any award as I was of that one. It is, unquestionably, the ugliest (its base is made of brown plastic) trophy in my collection, but it is still my favorite.

My third race of the year was at Lake Murray, where I had my first altercation on the racecourse. Altercations were pretty common at that time; some were because of poor-handling runabouts and were accidental. Others were not so accidental and just accepted as part of the competition. My first such incident was probably a little of both. The water that day was very rough, with numerous turnovers. This was perfect water for the old Doler, because of its weight and, of course, the side fins (which also served as bumpers). All the other Class A runabouts were smaller and much lighter, so I did enjoy a distinct advantage in this choppy water. While entering the first turn, I got into it with Buddy Lane from Texas, who came up on the short end of the stick. Fortunately, my "gunboat" was unscathed, and I finished second that day. Lane had a gaping hole in the front of his Winters hull and had to hobble in after the incident.

When I pulled into the pits after the heat, a big guy from Lane's crew was there to meet me. He promptly informed me that I couldn't drive a nail, and he was planning to beat the hell out of me. About that moment, a big voice from up on the hill boomed "Let that kid from Durant go." The fellow immediately released me and headed back to Lane's pit area. I looked up to see a big guy in a "man hat" asking me if I was okay. This was my first meeting with the racing legend Hi Drummond, who then bought me a hamburger. Hi was to become a good friend over the next few years.

The pits at Lake Murray, Oklahoma, in July 1952. This scene was typical of the postwar regattas, when docks and catwalks were often used by racers. The boats at that time were much sturdier than the featherweight hulls used by drivers in recent years and consequently accepted more abuse from the docks and other boats docked nearby. In 1952, the stock and modified runabout classes, which were raced in the Southwest, were required to contain a front cockpit for a rider. However, racers were permitted to use a tonneau cover, which snapped over the front cockpit to reduce wind resistance and improve the hull's handling characteristics. (R.E. Thompson photo)

Drummond, in addition to being one helluva boat racer, was an interesting character. He lived in "the city of Cartwright," a bustling little metropolis located on the Oklahoma-Texas border, about fifteen miles from my home. Cartwright's claim to fame was that it contained twenty-seven buildings: twenty-six beer joints and one filling station (which sold beer to go). The county in Texas, across the river from Cartwright, was dry. It also was accessible to Perrin Air Force Base, so Cartwright became a very popular watering hole. Bootleg whiskey and moonshine liquor were also sold in great quantities in that area. All of this conspired to make Cartwright a powder keg, and it was similar to how one would visualize the Klondike during Gold Rush days. Weekends were particularly wild, with plenty of the "four Bs" keeping things riled up (beer, booze, brawls, and broads). Saturday and Sunday mornings were somewhat lethargic, as that was usually clean-up time, with repairs in process to replace broken windows, rebuilding chairs and tables, and mopping up the blood. Drummond owned and operated one of these twenty-six watering holes, which he named Betty's Place (after his wife). His establishment was as rough as any on the strip, but relatively good order was kept, probably due to Hi's reputation for being tough.

I spent a lot of time at Betty's Place, where Hi helped me tune the Merc A engine. He had always raced two-cylinder B Merc engines, which were similar, so he was able to provide some very helpful advice. When we were not working on motors, Hi was helping me with my shuffleboard prowess. In the early 1950s, just about every bar had shuffleboard tables. Gambling on shuffleboard games became a popular practice, so it was beneficial to be able to hold your own in this "sport." Thanks to the ability to practice every day on his own table, Hi became extremely adept at the game. Consequently, it was not uncommon to see him shoot games for $100 in his or another neighboring bar. For that matter, you might see him drive to the other side of the state to engage in a game with someone else with a big shuffleboard reputation. When we attended a boat race, Hi would generally more than cover his travel expenses with his board winnings. Whatever he won racing was just icing on the cake.

At Betty's Place, you could always meet interesting characters. One afternoon, a fisherman came in, relating the sighting of an alligator in a cove near Texoma's Denison Dam. As Lake Texoma is a bit far north for gators, this story intrigued me, and I immediately took off for home to get a boat to go gator searching. About two hours later, I returned with a buddy and an aluminum fishing boat. We stopped by Betty's Place, picked up a six-pack, and headed out on the search. We didn't find the gator (or anything else very interesting either), but we sure enjoyed the beer.

On the weekend following the Lake Murray race, I entered a race on Lake of the Pines near Daingerfield, Texas. Dallas Calhoun, who lived in Hugo, about fifty miles east of my hometown of Durant, invited me to trailer with him to the Daingerfield event. Dallas had a two-boat trailer and was only using the bottom rack, so we put ol' *If* up on top and took off early in the morning. On the way out of Hugo (around six in the morning), Dallas and his brother-in-law Red Walcott, who was to pit for us, stopped at a local bootlegger's establishment and purchased a large fruit jar full of homemade gin, which really packed a punch. Before we reached the Red River, about fifteen miles south of Hugo, Dallas and Red got into the gin. Not wishing to be antisocial, I participated in the gin activity when the jar was passed to me. By the time we reached the racecourse, the three of us had finished off the hooch and were feeling no pain. The races were a disaster, at least for us. Dallas accidently beached his boat during the races, and I ended up sixteenth in a field of sixteen boats. Around noon, we missed Red, and someone said that he had driven our tow car away from the lake. While we were scratching our heads, trying to figure out where he had gone, Red returned with just what we needed: another fruit jar, this time filled with moonshine. He told us that a spectator had given him the tip on where to find this beverage in the neighboring hills.

Following Dallas's beaching incident, the race officials (Herb Scales and Pop Willis) held a meeting in which they decided Dallas and I would be disqualified and asked to leave. When approached with this mandate, I was embarrassed and proceeded to load up. However, Dallas and Red were incensed and promptly threatened to whip all the officials. The county sheriff ended up getting into the melee, and we took off for home with Red and Dallas still talking about what a raw deal we got. This barrage of disparaging remarks about the officials was greatly enhanced by Red's moonshine. In reflecting on this trip, I don't know how we ever made it home that night. Needless to say, this was the last trip I made with the Hugo boys.

That humbling sixteenth-place finish at Daingerfield gave me the idea that ol' *If* was too big to be competitive in the 15-cubic-inch "A" class. I was pondering this when Hi Drummond mentioned that his old running mate, Marvin Turner, had a smaller A-class Doler runabout for sale. Marvin was another colorful character who lived in nearby Madill (about thirty miles away). We struck a deal, and I purchased the boat. Marvin was changing over to Class B, which would require a larger hull.

Before any money changed hands, I tested my A Merc on Marvin's boat. To purchase a boat after what happened next should have made me suspect my sanity. Marvin and I drove out to Little Glasses Cove on Lake Texoma, where Marvin and Hi generally tested, hooked up the engine, and I climbed in and roared off. The boat felt fast, as it was about seventy-five pounds lighter than *If,* although it did hop a bit. After driving down the cove a distance, I decided it was time to test the hull's turning ability. The next thing I knew, I was in the drink, but the boat was sitting upright about thirty feet away. The boat had performed a beautiful 360-degree flip, but the driver had not. Right then I should have told Marvin thanks but no thanks; however, I thought I could tame that bronc and paid him for it anyway. As you might imagine, I never did completely tame that boat, and it did go over a few other times, although it did perform pretty well at most races.

I competed in ten different events in 1952, the latter part of the season in the boat I had purchased from Marvin. One of the first races in which I drove the new boat was at Lake Heyburn, near Sapulpa, Oklahoma. When we arrived at that racecourse on Saturday evening before the race, some of the drivers had just finished testing. One of them was a kid about my age, Paul Moon. Paul lived in nearby Sand Springs; thus, he named his hull the *Miss SS* (for Sand Springs). It was a two-cockpit runabout, typical of the time, built by Bill Fredrick, an Oklahoma boatbuilder of some repute. Moon had crashed the boat while testing and, in so doing, had ripped a hole about a foot square on the hull's planing surface. There was no way it could be properly repaired by race time, so Paul's dad walked to the lake concessionaire's restaurant to inquire about any wood he might have for a patch. The concessionaire was only able to come up with a wooden apple crate, which was eagerly accepted.

Paul and his dad then took the crate apart, nailed the side

of the crate to the bottom of the *Miss SS,* and then sealed the repair with pieces of tar taken from the asphalt road. The next day the *Miss SS* fared surprisingly well, and Paul drove it with this impromptu patch the rest of the season.

My last race of the 1952 season was the first national championship event in which I competed. Held on Lake Dallas (just north of Dallas, Texas), September 27–29, this NOA (National Outboard Association) Division III (stock) Nationals boasted over three hundred boats parked along that lake's sandy shore. I had no business being there, as my equipment was just plain outclassed. However, this event was held only a hundred miles from my home, so I wasn't going to let the opportunity of competing in such a race slip away. It turned out that I should have left my A rig at the house and just watched, as I ended up dead last in my qualifying heat!

Although I didn't fare well, I did gain some valuable experience and got to see one helluva show. I was extremely impressed by the performance of one Bob Terry of Jacksonville, Florida, who copped three of the nine championships at stake. Terry drove a new Swift hydro to two of these wins. It was our first look at this innovative hull, which was built in Mt. Dora, Florida, fairly close to Terry's home. Another impressive performance was turned in by Buddy Lane, the same guy I had tangled with earlier that season at Lake Murray.

A noteworthy finish came from John Jordan, a farmer from Kansas, who placed in the runner-up spot of the very competitive "B" Runabout event. What made John's accomplishment so special was that he drove all-aluminum boats. His hulls, a runabout and a hydro, had been built by the Blue Star Boat Company of Miami, Oklahoma. John was a regular on our Oklahoma circuit, and he was always a tough competitor in those light aluminum boats. I believe his two boats were the only racing hulls I ever saw skinned by aluminum, although I understand a few others were built at a later date.

Start of the Class B Runabout race at the 1952 NOA Stock Nationals. This is an interesting photo because it displays two unique hull designs that had not previously been seen by many who attended the event. One was the K51A boat, an all-aluminum hull driven by John Jordan (who finished second), and the other, H80, a round-chine hull driven by Jan Rinker. A second round-chine hull, piloted by an unidentified driver, is shown just behind Jordan. The aluminum boat's performance was impressive, but few of these hulls were ever built. However, the round-chine hulls, termed layover boats, later became very popular in the APBA stock ranks. Most of the boats raced in the A and B Runabout classes in the Southwest at that time were the Morphews and Winters, such as the 10To shown here driven by Stanley Henderson. (R.E. Thompson photo)

During the 1952 season, I received my first exposure to hydroplanes. Although our circuit was primarily devoted to runabouts we did stage a few Class B hydroplane heats that year. After watching these pancake-looking boats perform, I decided I couldn't live without one and ended up purchasing a used Winters hydro that had been campaigned the previous season by Deanie Montgomery. This boat, named *Special Delivery,* was a bit heavy for my A engine, but it handled well, and I did okay. However, it was never a front runner. (It probably needed a B engine to really make it go.)

At Cleburne, Texas, a few miles south of Fort Worth, Texas, the 1953 season kicked off in April. We had quite a trip en route to the race, as my pit crew that day was my dad and his lifelong friend Cecil Maxey. He was a huge fellow who was well known in our hometown for football prowess during his six- or seven-year tenure in high school. He really enjoyed sports but never much liked the academic part of school. "Maxey" was the city street commissioner and a real character. He and Dad kept me in stitches all the way to Cleburne that morning, telling stories about the old days.

I can remember one of the stories concerned the time that Maxey went with my parents on their honeymoon. My parents' destination was Niagara Falls, and Maxey rode with them as far as Detroit, where he was to pick up a new car to drive home. When they arrived within a few blocks of the auto plant, Maxey asked Dad to stop at a greasy-looking hamburger joint. After spending a few minutes in that establishment, he emerged with a sack full of burgers, a dozen to be exact, as the café had advertised a special price if sold by the dozen. Maxey then picked up the new car and drove over a thousand miles home nonstop, eating hamburgers all the way.

At the Cleburne event, I placed second in the runabout race but was disqualified for jumping the starting gun. It was a close call, but Dad and I accepted it as one of those racing deals. However, Maxey was livid. He claimed that the real reason for the disqualification was that I was an Okie. He further claimed that had I been from south of the Red River, as were the other drivers, I would have received the second-place award. He was ready to do battle with the officials, but Dad and I finally got him in the car, and we took off for home. All we heard on the way back was how the dirty Texans had cheated us. Maxey weighed about 250 pounds and had an appetite to match. He was especially fond of hamburgers and would usually eat two or three at a sitting. Dad felt that Maxey would calm down if we stopped along the way and bought burgers and fries. This ploy wasn't successful, however, as Dad and I got the burgers, but Maxey refused to eat because he would not buy anything in the state of Texas!

One of the early races in 1953 was at the Altus City Reservoir in the southwestern corner of Oklahoma. This was always an enjoyable annual event. I can especially remember the 1953 race, as that was my first glimpse of one of the infamous Hi Drummond–Dutch Cunningham altercations. Only one road, a single-lane dirt affair, led to the lake where the race was being held. This regatta always drew a big crowd, and that year was no different. About 11:00 a.m., as the crowd was driving in the gate, I heard quite a commotion; horns were honking and people were yelling in the direction of the entrance road. I walked up to the top of the lake's dam, where I could view the happenings, in time to see a car, belonging to Hi Drummond, parked in front of a line of cars. The big man from Cartwright was standing beside his car, waving a hatchet at a vehicle behind him owned by one Dutch Cunningham. Dutch was beside his car, brandishing a big ball-peen hammer, which he was waving at Hi. Both were yelling insults at the other and hurling numerous threats of violence. There were about five cars between them, and their passengers were horrified. Behind Dutch's car were probably fifty cars parked with their owners, mostly shocked, who were either honking their horns or had just rolled up their windows, locked their doors, and hidden in their seats. This violent scene continued for ten or fifteen minutes, until the local sheriff arrived. He, too, appeared somewhat apprehensive upon seeing these two madmen, but he was finally able to get Hi and Dutch to put away their weapons and proceed to the race site.

I later learned that Hi and Dutch were best of friends and just staged these encounters to add to the show. I was glad to learn that the threats were phony a few weeks later at a race in Wewoka, Oklahoma, where I was pitted between them. The pair staged another hatchet-and-hammer affair while they were standing waist-deep in water with me between them. The crowd was not aware that the duel was a phony and really got into it, yelling support for one or the other. I often wondered what people said after seeing one of our shows with a Hi-Dutch ordeal thrown in.

The D Runabout race was always a thriller. This photo depicts two Fort Worth, Texas, drivers setting up for a turn. Driving the Rooter Scooter boat, a Mercury KG9 powered Willis, is Jack Frank Crutcher. The Eight Ball hull, also a Willis, is driven by Jimmy Morrow. (R.E. Thompson photo)

July Fourth weekend that year was a busy one, with a race at Pawnee, Oklahoma, on the fourth (a Saturday) and at McAlester, Oklahoma, one hundred miles away, on the fifth. As Pawnee was a good driving distance from Durant, I traveled to Pawnee on the third and checked into the Palace Hotel (which was about the only place to stay in town). I'll never forget that evening, which was especially warm. The hotel had no air conditioning, and I had to leave the window wide open. I fell asleep early but was awakened about midnight with the worst racket imaginable just outside my window (which overlooked the tin roof of the building next door). The moon was full, so I was able to see plainly the cause of the noise. There must have been a hundred of the largest rats ever seen, running around on that tin roof. The screen on my window was in poor shape, with a few tears in it, so I had to shut the window to assure that the rats didn't enter, and had to spend one of the warmest and most miserable nights of my life.

The following day, the races were held without too much problem. A cash purse was advertised for the winners, but when payoff time approached, the paymaster could not be found. In those days, you were always paid for winnings in cash after the last race of the day. I usually relied on the prize money I won to buy fuel to get home. (Sometimes this didn't work out so well, so I occasionally had to borrow a few bucks to get on the road.) Unfortunately for the sponsors of the race, our referee, Harry Atkins, had been in the bottle during the event and was feeling no pain. I learned later that Harry, a reformed alcoholic, drank one day a year—always on the Fourth of July. Harry was the person delegated to collect prize money from the sponsors. He became very upset when he learned the purse had mysteriously disappeared. Harry, being incensed, promptly told the sponsoring group (a local civic organization) that the boat racers would take the town apart if the money was not received. The sponsoring group then left to search for the funds, while Harry led a group of the drivers to the county courthouse, located in the center of town.

I was late getting my equipment loaded and leaving the lake, so I was unaware of these monetary problems. On the way out of town, we had to drive by the courthouse. I was surprised to see about twenty racing rigs parked around the town square, near the courthouse, with Harry and several others threatening to empty the courthouse of its furniture and other items. Harry, I believe, had called a moving van from Tulsa, which was to pick up this stuff.

Shortly afterward, one of the members of the sponsoring group arrived with a money belt containing the racing purse. He related that the fellow responsible had gotten drunk and gone home with the cash in a money belt he was wearing. He was found in bed, passed out, with the belt still around his waist. This find saved the day, and we all headed out for McAlester for the next racing war.

There were a lot of stories about Harry Atkins's July 4 adventures. He was a great guy, and he led a completely normal life 364 days a year, but on July 4, you never knew what he was going to do. The previous year (1952), the Oklahoma Boat Racing Association had staged a show at Branson, Missouri, on July 4. A disappointing boat turnout of only seven rigs was on hand for the event. The prize money, around $2,000, was split among the seven drivers, and all seven ran in every heat. Harry and the announcer, Bill Adams, a deputy sheriff who weighed about three hundred pounds, put on quite a show, despite the small field of entries. Both got intoxicated (and I think some of the drivers did also) and used a great deal of imagination to entertain the large crowd on hand who had never seen a boat regatta. To interest the crowd and prevent confusion as to why the same boats ran in all the different classes, Adams would announce that, after each heat, the drivers and their crews would modify their engines and change their fuel mixtures. I guess it all worked, as Branson held another regatta the following year, but with another racing club responsible for the event.

Following the Branson race, all seven trailers headed back

for Oklahoma, with Harry and Adams leading the pack. While traveling through the Ozark Mountains, Harry spied a forest ranger's tower. He pulled over, and he and some of the others (who were also several sheets to the wind) climbed up the tower with the starting gun (a ten-gauge shotgun conversion). Harry then fired a ten-gun salute to all the boys who had fought in the Korean War. You just never knew what Harry would do on Independence Day!

Start of the B Hydro event at the 1952 NOA National Stock Championships in Dallas, Texas. The leading boat is 561T driven by Don Nicholson of Corsicana, Texas. (R.E. Thompson photo)

A week after the Pawnee and McAlester events, I attended a race at Grapevine Lake, just north of Dallas, Texas. The Dallas-Fort Worth area had a lot of racing equipment at that time, and I think all of it showed up that day. I was lucky to finish seventh, behind six Winters runabouts. That weekend, I decided I had to have a Winters to be competitive with these guys. The Winters was a much lighter and more streamlined hull than my old Doler boat.

On July 19, my parents and I drove to Paris, Texas, to pick up a new Winters, trading in the old Doler. We then drove on east into Arkansas to race on Lake Greeson, an Arkansas Power Boat Association event. The lake was really in the boonies, as the area was very sparsely populated. Roads into that country were almost inaccessible, and I didn't see how we could draw much of a crowd. We arrived about midmorning on Sunday, the race day, to find one of the largest fields of boats I had seen that year—and nearly no spectators.

We launched the new boat, and I took her for a spin. It was much faster than the old Doler but didn't handle as well. After a few laps around the track, I pulled in, made a few adjustments, and waited for the show to begin. At exactly noon, we heard bells ringing over the hill behind our pit area. About ten minutes later, we saw a huge throng of spectators coming over the hill. Evidently, church had just turned out, and all the parishioners came to see the races. Most of them were barefoot, and very few drove cars. It reminded me of Al Capp's Dogpatch, but we didn't see any Daisy Maes in the crowd.

My first race in the new boat was a disaster. The engine slipped on the slick finish of the new boat's transom, causing me to flip over. I was right in the middle of a field of sixteen runabouts, so it was a little hairy for me. However, neither the racing rig nor I was damaged, so about the only thing injured was my pride (and that was easily mended). I can remember being ecstatic that the engine was okay. It was common at that time to crack a cylinder block when you turned over, as we all used open exhaust dumps, which permitted cold water to splash directly into the engine's hot exhaust ports.

Unfortunately, my turnover record in the new Winters hull was not a good one. The following weekend, at Lawton, Oklahoma, I flipped over again. Other than the turnover, I don't remember much about the Lawton race, but I do remember the trip to that race. The tow car at that time was a 1948 Pontiac woodie station wagon that we fondly named the "Wooden Wonder." It was extremely hot the day we left for the races, so Dad and I waited until after dark to begin the 120-mile trip. Of course, the Wooden Wonder lacked air conditioning. About halfway to Lawton, Dad said he had enjoyed the heat long enough, as we had both broken quite a sweat with all the windows wide open. The next thing I knew, Dad, who was driving, had opened his door and was still maintaining a sixty-mile-an-hour clip down US 70. I promptly followed suit, and I suppose we made quite a sight, but we did cool down a bit.

A view of the race crowd at Lake Murray, Oklahoma, in July 1952. Races held during that time often drew large crowds of spectators as well as participants. At many events (usually held on Sundays), spectators would show up after church in their Sunday best, including neckties, high-heel shoes, and hats. The walkway pictured here led to a large dock where most of the racing entries were tied. In the foreground is shown a class-B modified engine, which was campaigned by Hi Drummond, a tough man to beat. Note the Johnson overhead fuel tank and Vacturi carburetor on Drummond's KG7 Mercury motor. (R.E. Thompson photo)

The 1953 season ended in Oklahoma with the National Outboard Association (NOA) Zone Championships, held at Lake Hulah near Bartlesville. The winners qualified for a starting berth in the NOA Division IV (Modified Outboard) Nationals, to be held in early October at Hot Springs, Arkansas. I didn't fare too well, as the new Winters took its third bath of the year. I did end up going to the nationals, however, but as a spectator, with old comrade Marvin Turner.

The next year, 1954, was another busy season for the Oklahoma Boat Racing Association and the nation in general. As in the previous year, I competed in both the A Hydro and Runabout classes in Oklahoma and Texas. I also drove a short while that year for Jack Logan who owned a "B" rig. My younger brother Hal was to pit for me that year, and he accompanied me to the season opener at Altus, Oklahoma. Hal, whose nickname was Red, had bright-red hair and a fair complexion to go with it. I'll never forget the Altus race, as I've never seen anyone get as sunburned as he did that day. Of course, sunscreen was not yet available, so with no shade in sight, we were completely at the mercy of the sun.

I fared pretty well at the races that day and picked up my prize money at the end of the event. Neither Red nor I had eaten all day, so we looked forward to dinner as soon as we left the lake. A greasy-spoon cafe was located at the edge of town, so we went in to eat and take a boat racer's bath (which was performed in the sink of the men's restroom). When we were seated at our table, we looked over the menu, and I opted for a steak, since I was feeling rich. Red said he would also like a steak dinner. My brother, who was about thirteen years old at the time, was a little on the pudgy side. This fact prompted me to say to the waitress, "Bring me one of your steak dinners, and bring the fat boy a hamburger." The pathetic thing here was that I actually thought a hamburger was less fattening than a steak and that I was doing Red a favor. However, he didn't see it that way, became livid, and wouldn't talk to me all the way home. This race (and the subsequent dinner) turned out to be my pit man's last that year, for which I could not fault him. When we arrived home, Dad learned the dinner story from Red (who embellished it somewhat), and it was logged in as one of those all-time family stories that family members never let me forget.

During the 1954 season, I became well acquainted with the Miller family, with whom I am still close friends. Kenneth Miller and Pete Norton were teammates at that time. Kenneth drove a Speedliner runabout named *Lazy Mama,* while Pete chauffeured a Class B Swift hydro. Both were good competitors, and Pete won the NOA Division IV (Modified) Nationals that year. When I think of Pete, I always recall his trip to Mexico, which occurred one summer when I was pumping gasoline in Dad's service station. Pete was on his way home to Vinita, Oklahoma, from the trip when he stopped by to purchase gas and say hello. Pete was driving a brand-new Cadillac, which I was admiring, when he told me to look in the back. Pete had removed the rear seat, which he left in Mexico. In its place were two huge pottery urns, each filled to the brim with tequila. This was significant, as in 1954, Oklahoma was a dry state. Had Pete been caught transporting that much liquor, he would probably have received a life jail sentence. He didn't seem to be concerned about that, however, as he figured he could outrun anybody in that new Caddy.

Pete's partner, Kenneth Miller, was a great guy and generally brought his family with him on the circuit. Mrs. Miller (Marie) was a super lady who, at the Lawton race, I found to be both a compassionate person and a great cook. I arrived at the Lawton race site early in the morning with an empty stomach. It was a long way to the nearest restaurant, so I grabbed a few grocery staples (a sack of potato chips and a bottle of strawberry pop) at a nearby gas station. At the lake, I was met with the wonderful smell of bacon frying and coffee brewing, all emanating from the Miller-Norton pit area. I had no choice but to put on my hungriest face and walk around their trailer with an occasional glance at the meal preparations. It all worked, and Mrs. Miller asked me to participate. This was the first of several such meals I enjoyed during the next couple of years. The Millers' oldest son was a redheaded kid named Leonard a couple of years younger than me. Kenneth bought Leonard a Class A Swift hydro, which he drove quite well. The Millers quit racing in the mid-1950s, but Leonard returned to the sport ten years later and competed in several different classes until the early 1990s. A third-generation Miller, Leonard's son Rick, began racing in the late 1970s and still competes very successfully. In recent years, a fourth-generation Miller by the name of Braxton began racing and is now a very competitive driver.

One race I won't forget, held in early June 1954, occurred at Wewoka, Oklahoma. Marvin Turner accompanied me on this trip, which probably should never have occurred. Still, I did win a first place. It all started when ol' Marvin wanted to stop at the first tavern just outside his hometown of Madill, Oklahoma. This stop became the first of many between Madill and Wewoka, about eighty-five miles away. We were both in poor shape by the time we reached our destination and checked into the luxurious Hotel Wewoka (probably a boarding house for welfare recipients that was made available, at special rates, to boat racers that weekend).

Prior to our departure, I had made a date with a girl I had met in college who, at the time, was visiting a friend in a nearby town some fifteen miles from Wewoka. When Marvin and I arrived at the hotel, I lay down in the room to rest and fell fast asleep. I was awakened about midnight by quite a commotion outside my second-floor window. The room wasn't air conditioned, and I had left the window wide open, so none of the noise was filtered. When peering out, I was shocked to see what seemed like the entire Oklahoma Boat Racing Association engaged in one helluva party on the street. Marvin, who was really inebriated at the time, spied me at the window and extended an invitation to attend the "inauguration," to celebrate the group's appointment of the new town officials, Mayor Harry Atkins, Sheriff Clyde Bayer, and other boat racing dignitaries who had been self-appointed to various "official capacities." It was quite a party, and the street had been blocked off with racing rigs parked in every direction.

I informed Marvin I had a date and intended to keep it. He claimed I was in no condition to drive and informed me he intended to do the driving and grabbed the car keys. We unhooked the trailer, got a couple more beers (which was just what we needed), and started out in my Pontiac woodie for Seminole, where my date was located. It was obvious neither of us should have been driving, and this became quite clear when we realized neither of us knew where we were going. In an attempt to negotiate a curve in the road, Marvin ran off the highway, and the woodie came to an abrupt halt in a bar ditch. The next thing I knew was that Marvin had passed out cold. The Wooden Wonder was stuck in the ditch on high center, with no traffic to flag down for help. I hoofed it a couple of miles to the nearest farmhouse. When I banged on the door, I received the kind of reception you might expect to receive from a farmer who has been awakened by a drunk at 2:00 a.m. I was, in no uncertain terms, instructed to vacate the premises immediately, and if not, I could expect to see the barrel of his shotgun and the teeth of his dog. I promptly retreated in fast order and returned to the Wooden Wonder, where Marvin was enjoying a wonderful rest. I finally was able to hitch a ride into town in the back of a produce truck, found a wrecker, and had the Wooden Wonder pulled out of the ditch (with Marvin still asleep in it). When we finally rolled back into town, the sun was just peeking over the horizon. Marvin then woke up and asked, "Where are we?" I could have shot him!

1952 pit scene at Casino Beach on Lake Worth, in Fort Worth, Texas. Depicted in this shot are mostly Willis, Morphew, and Winters boats. All three of these hulls were built in the state of Texas. The Lake Worth races were always held early in the year, and a large number of entries were always drawn from Oklahoma and Texas. During that era, there were

enough race boats located in the Dallas-Fort Worth
complex alone to stage a very large regatta. (R.E.
Thompson photo)

During the 1954 season, my interests began to gravitate
toward the larger-horsepower classes. The A and B classes were
great, but the faster speeds and sounds of the larger engines,
especially the high-pitched whine of the four-cylinder Mercs,
finally got to me. At that time, the Oklahoma Boat Racing
Association was conducting races for the D Class Runabout
but not the hydroplane. However, the four-cylinder D-Class
Mercury on a hydroplane was permitted to compete in the wild
Free for All event that always ended the day's racing program.
In nearby Texas, the D Hydros were already appearing on their
race schedules, and it looked as if the class was destined for
Oklahoma in 1955. I decided it was time to move up, so I sold
my entire rig to Garland Peterson, an Okie from Muskogee
(literally), and I purchased a Merc 40H Class D engine and
Willis hydro in Texas. I was really looking forward to the 1955
season.

As was customary, the 1955 OBRA season opener was held
at Altus, Oklahoma, on the city reservoir where I entered the
D Hydro and Free for All events. Since this was my first race
in the new rig, I was pretty excited. As this was the first OBRA
scheduled D Hydro event, we only had a handful of boats in
the race. The new boat ran well, and I fared okay, though I can't
recall what place I finished. The Free for All was a different story.
Most of the entries were runabouts powered by the old opposed-
cylinder 33- and 50-horsepower mills and a few of the newer
four-cylinder Mercurys. There were three or four Mercury D

hydros and one old opposed-cylinder C hydro (which I figured was the least of the competition).

My experience that day taught me to never underestimate anyone. Though I had speed on the runabouts, they worked me over, as they could out turn and out handle my ten-foot hydro. Their hulls were thirteen feet long and weighed about twice as much as mine. I think I finished last or close to it that day. The big surprise, however, was that old opposed-cylinder C hydro rig that ran off and hid from everyone. I later learned that the old C was not powered by a service engine, to which I was accustomed, but a PR "hexhead" professional alky-burning mill driven by a fellow from Midland, Texas, by the name of Hap Sharp. The engine had been built by one of the best motor men ever, Frank Vincent, and it was run on a brand-new Neal hydro. This same rig won the NOA Free for All National Championship later that year.

Hap Sharp was an interesting figure. His parents had been involved in boat racing for several years, and his mother had been a Midget Class champion in the Professional ranks. Hap's father had owned a huge drilling company in Midland, a west Texas town known for its abundance of oil and millionaires. Hap competed in regattas all over the United States and later competed in big-time auto racing, teaming up with Jim Hall of Indy car fame. After retiring from racing, Hap's interest turned to polo, and he purchased a South American national polo team; their playing field was the world. To transport the ponies, I was informed that Hap purchased a Boeing jetliner; Hap always did things first class! Though it's been many years since I've seen Hap, I viewed him on film on three occasions this past year: once on a video rerun of the 1949 Albany-New

York Marathon and twice on ESPN reruns on sports-car races from the 1960s. He had won both races, one at Watkins Glen.

I attended some great races in 1955. One event that stands out in my memory was held on Caddo Lake, a few miles north of Shreveport, Louisiana. This was a large lake full of cypress trees in the heart of a very prolific oilfield. A large entry list of some of the hottest Modified and Professional drivers in the country was on hand. The Shreveport area was a hotbed of alky burners, boasting such standouts as Bubba Haley, the LaFitte Brothers, Ted Lewis, Harry Marioneaux, and others who had gained national recognition. It was also the home of, in my opinion, the greatest propeller man of all time, R. Allen "Poppa" Smith, a legendary figure.

Because of an engine problem, I sat out the day but witnessed an awesome show, particularly in the Free for All event. Raymond Owen from Fort Worth, Texas, the 1953 and 1954 NOA D Modified Hydro champion, was in the field, along with one of the biggest names in the business, Bob McGinty, driving the Allen Smith–prepared Marioneaux equipment. Henry Grupe, a widely known Professional C hop-up artist, was eager to prove the PR was still the engine to beat, so he brought a stable of drivers from Dallas, Texas, to put it on Raymond. It turned out to be quite a show, with the Grupe drivers boxing Owen in at the start and wetting him down. A PR was a tough engine for a Merc to beat, before exhaust pipes were developed, and Grupe had some of the best around. However, the PR boys were so busy with Raymond, they overlooked a big Ashburn hydro powered by a D Merc from Houston, Texas, driven by a veteran of the tough Lone Star circuit by the name of O.B. Aylor. He ran up through the pack, and those who got in his way regretted it, as he made the wood chips fly. Aylor ended up winning that day in one of the most unusual-looking hydros I've ever seen.

After the races, I had to go take a closer look at this amazing boat, owned by a fellow named Sabara. The hull was huge by 1955 standards, and this was the first hydro I had seen that had a wooden skin on its nose instead of the standard aircraft linen. The hull had plenty of battle scars, which was typical of a Lone Star boat, and the engine was so rusty, I was amazed it would run at all, much less accomplish what it had just done. In the boat's cockpit, by the steering wheel, was a carved ivory idol for good luck.

Raymond Owen, the 1953 NOA Division 4 D Hydro National champion, is shown in his winning Willis hydroplane, powered by a Mark 40H modified Mercury. Like most hulls of that era, this one was short (only ten feet long), built with a mahogany plank bottom. During his ten years in racing, Raymond was an extremely tough driver to beat. He retired from the sport in the early 1960s after suffering a couple of serious racing injuries. Owen always kept immaculately clean equipment and once told me that if two boats were identical, one clean and one dirty, the clean one would win every time. Raymond is now retired from the Federal Aeronautic Administration and living on a ranch in central Texas. (R. E. Thompson photo)

Following the races, I trailered back to Fort Worth, Texas, with Raymond Owen, Jimmy Epperson, and Ed Harrison. I was to start a new job in a marine dealership there the following day. Everything was going okay until we got to Wills Point, Texas, a few miles east of Dallas. There in the road were several of the Dallas PR boys, signaling us to pull over to continue their encounter with Raymond, who was driving the lead vehicle. Raymond wisely continued his journey, picking up the pace a bit, and that was the last we saw of that group.

My move to Fort Worth that summer was an experience. I went to work for Virgil Vogt who, at that time, was the largest Yellow Jacket boat dealer in the United States and one of the largest Mercury Outboard dealers in the country. My job was rigging boats, which I did until the fall, when I returned to college at the University of Oklahoma. My recollection is that I rigged or helped rig a majority of the more than fifty fourteen-foot Yellow Jackets with Mercury Mark 55 outboard motors that Virgil sold that summer.

My stay in Fort Worth afforded me the opportunity to race in the north Texas and Oklahoma area every weekend and to become acquainted with a large number of members of the Dallas and Fort Worth racing fraternity. In the 1950s, that area was a real hotbed of boat-racing activity. Most of the drivers belonged to either the Dallas Boat Club or the Cowtown Outboard Club in Fort Worth. The Dallas club boasted members such as Pop and Ken Willis (builders of the Willis boats), Henry Grupe (the engine builder), Phil Crown (the 1959 NOA C Runabout champion), Doc Ramsey, G. G. Slack (the 1952 NOA C champion), and the Henderson Brothers, whose offspring, Denny and Stanley, and a grandson Bruce until recently were still in the racing business.

The Cowtown club had its share of top contenders too. Some of its members were Raymond Owen, a fearsome driver who won several NOA world or national titles, two of the hottest two-cylinder drivers in the late 1950s, Jimmy Epperson and Ed Harrison, and Richard McCulloch (whose father built the Cencro Tone exhaust system). Other outstanding competitors included Doc Owen, Joe Shertliff, Doug Delap, Gerald Newton, W. O. Thompson, and Pop and Jack Crutcher. I didn't belong to either club but would attend the Cowtown club meetings, with Jimmy and Raymond, which were always held at the Newton Ranch, north of Fort Worth.

Races were held weekly in the north Texas area, and large crowds of entries and spectators were the norm. All events were sanctioned by the National Outboard Association (NOA), and starting fields were limited to sixteen boats. Elimination heats were often required, and most of the competition was fierce. A majority of the boats were still runabouts in the mid-1950s, but the hydro fields were growing. Most of the smaller-class boats (A and B) were Winters. A majority of the larger-class boats were Willis, built in Dallas, though a few Speedliners and others could also be seen. In 1955, the engines were modified, and most ran on methanol fuel, with castor oil used for the lubricant. There is nothing I know of that smells better than burning castor oil, an aroma I have missed dearly for several years.

Raymond Jeffries, a Texan, was one of the toughest competitors I've ever seen. He is pictured here in the mid-1950s behind the wheel of a homemade runabout (possibly built by himself) powered by a modified KG9 Mercury engine. Raymond did everything himself, including boat and engine building, and he even pitched his own props. Raymond's equipment was not the best looking but would run with the best. His shortcoming was undoubtedly sign painting, as is evidenced by the numbers on this hull. Raymond was known to walk the banks after a race to collect any engine part that had been discarded, including spark plugs. These parts usually found their way to Raymond's engine the following week. (Photo origin unknown)

One race I can remember in 1955, which I would prefer to forget, occurred at Lake Overholser in Oklahoma City. Brother Red and I drove up from Durant that morning, stopping to pick up our old buddy Marvin Turner in Madill. Marvin was ready to go when we arrived wearing his wading shoes and toting a bottle of booze. That's when I made my first mistake of the day by not turning around and driving back home. The next 120 miles to Oklahoma City were spent dusting off Marvin's refreshment. Marvin had the lion's share of the bottle, but I must admit I helped a little. By the time we reached the outskirts of Oklahoma City, Marvin's "medicine bottle" was empty, and he was still thirsty. I was directed to a bootlegger Marvin knew and, within a few minutes, a new jug was in his possession. By the time we arrived at the race site, Marvin was in rare form, and I must admit I wasn't feeling much pain either.

I don't remember much about the races that day, but I know I didn't haul home any cash or hardware. I do recollect that things got worse as the day progressed. Following the races, the Overholser Motor Boat Club (OMBC), a cosponsor of the event, always held a big feed, and that year was no different. We all trailered over to the OMBC clubhouse, about a mile up the lake from the race site. By that time, Marvin was somewhat in a state of euphoria, having emptied the second bottle we had purchased that morning. When we arrived at the clubhouse, the food was already being served, and unfortunately, a keg of beer had been tapped, and its contents were going fast.

Brother Red and I were standing on the boat dock with

plates of food in our hands when out of the blue charges Marvin. His eyes were so bloodshot, I don't know if he knew who he was attacking, but nevertheless, he was intent on throwing me into the lake. Fortunately, I saw him in time to step to one side, while Marvin vaulted headfirst into the drink. We helped him back onto the dock, but as soon as he cleared the water, he grabbed me in an attempt to get me wet. Red came to my rescue, jumping on Marvin's back, trying to restrain him. Up to that point, everyone else in attendance was watching the festivities, but now the game changed. Suzie Hammon, whose husband, Mike, was one of the local drivers (and who was almost in the same condition as Marvin), decided that ol' Marvin needed help and evened up the odds by jumping on Red. This turn of events prompted a few other drivers to join the action, and the matter turned into a full-scale brawl. The next thing I knew, we were being put under arrest by the police. Fortunately, one of the officers was a friend of Mike Hammon's, who was able to talk him out of the arrest, promising that all concerned would behave and lay off the beer. I figured we had better get the hell out of Dodge, and we left. Before passing the city limits, Marvin was sawing logs and dreaming of his former boat-racing glories.

By the time the 1956 season rolled around, I was ready to go with a remodified 40H Merc. By this time, the engine had been internally modified, an opposed-cylinder Johnson tank mounted for gravity feed, and a pair of 33-horsepower Evinrude carburetors bored out for alcohol had been mounted. Also, several cans of Chris Go racing fuel had been stocked for the season. Unfortunately, the additional speed obtained by the engine changes, plus the higher center of gravity caused by the overhead tank, put the performance of my ten-foot hydro on the wild side. As a result, I became one of the leading members of the submarine club that season, with several dunkings. My last flip of the year occurred at Canton Lake, Oklahoma, where I ended up in the hospital with a bruised spleen after stuffing the Willis. Not all the season was wet, however, and we did have our moments, racing mostly in Oklahoma and occasionally Texas that year.

In the fall of that year, I met Ken Parks, who had just finished his rookie year with the OBRA. Ken continued racing since that time and, until recent years, was still an active driver. Ken, Bill Lavery, and I attended a professional regatta on Lake Texoma that I remember vividly. Lavery had just acquired a Johnson PR 65, which he entered in the C Hydro event, and Ken and I pitted for him. That day, I was awed by the Marioneaux-McGinty contingent in a display I'll never forget.

Early that morning, the huge Marioneaux trailer pulled into the pits, driven by several members of the Marioneaux crew. Harry Marioneaux, owner of the racing stable, was a wealthy Shreveport, Louisiana, businessman who was principal stockholder and CEO of the Brewster Company, a huge manufacturer of offshore drilling rigs. Harry had immaculately prepared equipment, all new Neal hydros and Desilva runabouts. All the Marioneaux engines (PRs, SRs, KRs, C Service, etc.) were the finest built by Harry's employee, none other than R. Allen "Poppa" Smith. Needless to say, Harry had quite an arsenal of propellers all built by Mr. Smith, probably the best wheel man ever. Harry's driver was a very talented Bob McGinty, a former Lone Star circuit driver from Corpus Christi, Texas.

After the Marioneaux rig arrived, we watched its crew set up a boat for every class scheduled that day. Following the setup activity, one of the crew members tested each boat, and certain propeller and set-up changes were made. All the boats and engines were then wiped down, and the crew waited.

About noon, an amphibious airplane flew overhead, tipping its wings hello. It then circled and landed on the lake, pulling up to the Marioneaux pits. Harry, McGinty, and a pilot stepped out and walked on the sponsons to the shore without ever getting wet. McGinty barely made the drivers' meeting scheduled for noon. Following the meeting, McGinty put on his helmet and life jacket and was carried to the boat he was to drive in the first heat. One of the crew pulled the cord, and the engine started immediately. Bob McGinty won that heat. In fact, I believe he won every heat of the entire event. After each race, he was carried to the next boat on the schedule and didn't have to get wet all day. Following the last heat of the day, the pilot fired up the plane, Harry and Bob jumped in, and away they roared. The three of us could just stare with our mouths wide open, never having seen anything like what we had just witnessed. After the plane departed, the crew dismantled and loaded all the equipment and headed back to Shreveport. What a deal!

At the end of the 1956 season, I was beginning my senior year at the University of Oklahoma in Norman. Two years earlier, I had met the apple of my eye, a cute little brunette who was destined to change my entire future (which, up to that time, had been centered primarily on boat racing). At this time, I decided to go the shackles and bonded route and pop the big question; however, I didn't have a cent to purchase a ring. Unfortunately, the only thing of value I did own was—you guessed it, the D hydro rig. It was tough having to sell my racing equipment, but sometimes you just gotta do what you gotta do.

In April of the following year, Sandra and I were married, and my racing fever had to be put on hold for a while. During the 1957 and '58 seasons, I was transformed into a spectator, and Sandra and I attended several races as such. However, in 1958, the bug bit again, and I bought an old Mercury KG9 that was badly in need of some TLC (time, labor, and cash). At that time, we were living in Guthrie, Oklahoma, a small community north of Oklahoma City. I dismantled the old Mercury in my garage and began whittling on it.

Jimmy Nichols of Kansas City, Missouri, driving a new Speedliner Class D modified runabout in this 1959 photo. Jimmy was an excellent driver who competed successfully in almost every alky burner class.

One day that winter, I drove over to Cushing, a nearby town, to visit Bill Lavery. Bill had been heavily involved in racing that season, campaigning a class-C alky hydro named *Party Doll*. At one of the last races of the season, Bill had nearly destroyed the *Party Doll,* formerly a beautiful big C Neal hull. To make a long story short, I ended up hauling what was left of the *Party Doll* home that day. I still remember the puzzled look on Bill's face as I drove away. I'm sure he wondered what in the world I was going to do with that pile of kindling.

A month or so later, I entered a partnership with an old friend, Earl Nelson, with whom I had raced in the A runabout class a few years earlier. Earl agreed to provide the boat and trailer, while I was to furnish the propulsion. I offered the *Party Doll* remains to Earl, who was very skeptical that there was enough left of her to rebuild. However, we agreed to take the *Party Doll* to another old racing friend, Delbert Gann, who also lived in Guthrie. Delbert was a cabinetmaker by trade who had built a few boats himself. He was a real craftsman, so we knew if he decided to take on the project of rebuilding the *Party Doll,* it would be done right.

After looking over our wood pile, Delbert did reluctantly agree to tackle the project, and over the next few months, the old hull was transformed into a real work of art. It came out so well that it was placed in a boat show the following year. Earl and I campaigned that boat during the 1959, '60, and '61 seasons, with Earl doing the driving and me wrenching on the KG9.

THE SPORT CONTINUES

1960–1969

The 1960s started out with a bang when, on March 29, 1960, Hugh Entrop of Seattle, Washington, became the fastest outboard driver in history, clocking 114.65 mph at Lake Havasu, Arizona. This amazing feat was performed in a fourteen-foot, three-point Entrop-McDonald cabover hydro named *Starflite Too,* powered by a Jones-Hubbell prepared Evinrude.

At the beginning of the 1960s, the economy was still good, and the boating industry was experiencing a period of prosperity. However, as the decade wore on, the Vietnam War and other factors affected the sport, resulting in a drop in participation and diminished spectator counts. The war was probably the primary reason for the downturn, as many of the younger competitors were being drafted. However, television and air conditioning in homes probably ran a close second. At that time, baseball was receiving the lion's share of the television market, and many of their games were played on Sundays, when most races were scheduled.

Hu Entrop of Seattle, Washington, is shown here working on his OMC V4 power plant at Guaymas, Mexico, in 1962. At that time, Hu was the World Unlimited Outboard speed record holder, a feat he had accomplished on three different occasions in 1958 and 1960. At this race in Guaymas, however, he had his hands full in the Free for All event with, of all things, an A hydro powered by a Konig alky engine, driven by Texan Jimmy Epperson. Jimmy got a head start in that race and could almost touch every buoy with his boat's uncanny ability to turn, whereas Entrop was forced to make large, sweeping turns with his unlimited rig. At each turn, Epperson was able to get inside and take the lead coming off the corner; Entrop would then overtake him on the straights. This seesaw battle lasted until the last lap, when Entrop finally prevailed by passing Epperson just before the finish line. (National Outboard Association photo)

In spite of these adverse conditions, there was still an abundance of racing. For example, in 1968, more than three hundred outboard racing events were sanctioned in the United States by the two major sanctioning bodies at that time, the American Power Boat Association (APBA) and the National Outboard Association (NOA). Approximately 64 percent of these races were primarily stock outboard events or at least included some stock outboard classes on the program, while 46 percent of the events included Professional (NOA) or Alky (APBA) classes. A quarter included events for the Amateur Division (NOA), later known as the Pleasure Boat Division or the Outboard Pleasure Craft Division (APBA). Ten percent of the races that year included Am Pro (NOA) classes. The largest gainer for the decade was in the pleasure boat area, where the major American outboard manufacturers were concentrating.

Throughout the decade, the majority of outboard racing continued to be centered in the APBA Stock Outboard category, where the largest group of that organization's memberships lay. Racing classes in that division remained pretty much the same as they had in the late '50s due to the sizes of the engines manufactured by Mercury. These were classes J (ten cubic inches), A (fifteen cubic inches), B (twenty cubic inches), C (thirty cubic inches), 36 (thirty-six cubic inches), and D (forty cubic inches). All these classes were Mercury affairs, except the 36, which never did quite gain the popularity of the other classes. The only new Mercury introduced into the Stock Outboard Division during the sixties was a J stock engine, which competed in the J class for novices. Though it produced no other new engines during the period, Mercury did continue to produce plenty of replacement parts for the stock outboard drivers, and supplies of these items was not a problem.

During the 1960s, the American outboard manufacturers were concentrating their production in accordance with consumer demands, which dictated larger, more powerful engines. These newer models were raced in the pleasure boat divisions of both the APBA and the NOA in their "factory stock" condition.

The early years of pleasure boat racing were somewhat similar to the infant stages of stock outboard racing, in that a contestant could use his family ski or fishing boat to compete in a regatta, and the technical rules were established accordingly. However, during the 1960s, these boats became more specialized, and by the end of the decade, they had evolved into performance hulls that could easily outperform the standard "family" boat. Most of the early pleasure boat racers drove strictly production engines, but as this segment of racing seasoned, the engine manufacturers began producing specialized mills to meet the growing demand for them. Pleasure boat racing, which later evolved into OPC (outboard performance craft) racing is a story in itself that I will not try to cover in this writing. In the 1960s, this type of racing was in its infancy and, like stock outboard racing in the 1950s, received its lifeblood from the engine manufacturers.

John Jordan was a great competitor. Here he is shown in 1961 with the Texas State Championship trophies he won in the C Class hydroplane and runabout classes. At that time, John was driving for Brady Marine of San Antonio, Texas. That same year, at St. Paul, Minnesota, John also won the NOA World Championships in these same classes, driving the T606 boats shown here. John's racing debut was in the early 1950s, at which time he was a Kansas wheat farmer. He piloted the first aluminum racing boat I ever encountered, a Blue Star brand built in Miami, Oklahoma. (Photo origin unknown)

Almost half of all outboard events in the United States during the decade included racing events for the professional or alky engines. During the early part of the 1960s, the modified Mercurys were dominant in some classes, but the foreign-built Konigs and Anzanis were victorious in others. Also, modified versions of the little Champion Hot Rod, manufactured at that time by Swanson Outboard in Minneapolis, Minnesota, were also somewhat competitive.

To combat the foreign-engine influx, Quincy Welding of Quincy, Illinois, developed the Quincy Looper, a specialized racing mill that used some Mercury components such as crankshafts, lower units, tower housings, clamp-bracket assemblies, etc. The engines' blocks, reed cages, pistons, and other parts were manufactured by or for the Quincy concern. These motors turned out to be competitive with the foreign jobs. Another alky mill that made its presence known at that time was the Harrison, a limited-production engine produced by the Harrison family of Vermilion, Ohio, a well-known name in the alky circles for many years.

In the AmPro (American Professional) Division of the NOA, almost all of the engines raced were modified Mercs and Champion Hot Rods. The class designations followed the stock outboard guideline, e.g., A (fifteen cubic inches), B (twenty cubic inches), etc. However, an additional class designated as E was adopted for this racing category that covered the 44-cubic-inch Mercs (the 45-horsepower and 50-horsepower pleasure boat blocks). Also, a D-1 Class designation was established for the thirty-six-cubic-inch Evinrude and Johnson engines, but this was never considered a very popular class. Rules covering the Am Pro engines permitted only minor alterations from stock. These included limited porting of the blocks, the addition of any type of exhaust system, the use of a fabricated tower housing, and a few other incidental motor changes.

Dieter Konig and his bride, Eleanor, pose behind one of his creations, which he brought to the United States. This engine is mounted on a Big Bee Swift hull. Dieter made several trips to the United States during the late fifties and early sixties, to promote the Konig engines. The first time I saw him was at the 1959 NOA National Championships, where he competed in the Class C hydro event. (National Outboard Association photo)

Boats used in competition during the 1960s were somewhat improved over their 1950s counterparts. This improvement was the result of better designs, improved building methods, and an item commonly called a "rubbing board." The latter, technically termed as foam glass, an insulation material used in commercial freezer applications, began to be used with more frequency by boat owners to remove high spots from boat planing surfaces, which greatly improved their stability and speed. Foam glass was particularly useful on runabout hulls whose bottom surfaces were more sensitive to planing conditions.

During the early seasons of the decade, many hulls that had been built in the 1950s continued to be raced. These included the Desilvas, Neals, Fillingers, Sid Crafts, Pabsts, Swifts, Speedliners, Willis, and other lesser-knowns. As the decade wore on, Speedliners Pabsts, Desilvas, and Sid Crafts continued to be built. The Warren runabout became a competitive choice of several drivers during that time, and by the end of the period, the Staron had become a favorite. The Speedliner hull was discontinued during this period but was replaced by the Seajay, and the Sid Craft was replaced in the mid-1960s by the Sid Son. Several small boat builders also sprang up at that time, producing racing hulls bearing the names of Byers, Dubinski, and others that did well on the nation's racecourses. Plank boats, by that time, had all been replaced by plywood jobs that were much lighter and easier to build. Most hydros continued to be constructed with aircraft linen decks, but hard decks were beginning to appear on the newer boats.

As was the case with the boats and engines, the nation's drivers were also changing. Many of the top pilots of the fifties began their retirement in the early sixties and were replaced by a new generation of throttle jockeys. Bud Wiget was one of those retirees who decided to give up the outboard game in 1963 to begin racing inboards. Wiget was one of the greatest outboard drivers of all time, having accomplished just about everything possible during the 1940s and 1950s, including forty-two world speed records and numerous national championships. In 1961, Wiget was honored by being named to the APBA Honor Squadron, one of the sport's most prestigious awards.

There were some really outstanding drivers in the 1960s in all categories of outboard racing. Replacing the legendary Wiget, Creech, Tenny, Livingston, Torigiani, McGinty, and others familiar to race fans during outboard racing's golden years were newer names such as Jim Schoch, Billy Seebold Jr., Freddie Goehl, Dickie Pond, Bob Hering, Clayton Elmer, and numerous others in the alky ranks. In stock outboard racing, names such as Clark Maloof, Stover Hire, Fred Miller, and others were found synonymous with championships of the era. In the Am Pro category, it was Dick Aveline, Walter Courtois, Harry Brinkman, Willie Hobson, Emmet Homfeld, and others who posted the lion's share of victories.

Three of the "heavy hitters" of the 1960s era are pictured together in this 1965 photo taken at Knoxville, Tennessee. Nick Marchetti, the well-known boat builder, is in the center, flanked by Gerry Waldman (left) and Willie Hobson, two of the top drivers of the era. Waldman, the winner of numerous outboard championships, was considered an icon in the sport. A few years later, he was killed in a racing accident at Hot Springs, Arkansas. Hobson, one of the hottest pilots to emerge from the Indiana Outboard Association ranks, was a big winner in NOA championships. Both Hobson and Waldman drove boats built by Marchetti. (National Outboard Association photo)

We had a great time racing in the 1960s. At the beginning of the decade, Earl Nelson and I campaigned both a class-D alky hydro (the former *Party Doll*), and a D Runabout (an early model Ashburn). We didn't exactly set the world on fire but had one helluva good time. The Oklahoma Boat Racing Association was then scheduling a lot of races, so most of the events we attended were in state, and we generally pulled the racing trailer with Earl's Plymouth. (Earl was a carburetor specialist who was employed by a Chrysler-Plymouth dealer at that time.) We usually departed from Earl's house before dawn and returned late that evening. We were always accompanied by Earl's wife, Mary, and Joe Adair (or "Chief," as he was called). We generally enjoyed a lively conversation to and from the races, and the trip home was often spiced up by several brews. Prior to her marriage to Earl, Mary had been married to a musician in the Bob Wills western swing band, and we always heard a lot of stories about her days on the road with that musical group.

Often, Mike Hammon (then retired from racing) and his wife, Suzie, would accompany us. One amusing incident occurred when Mike and Suzie followed us to a race at Hominy in northeast Oklahoma. During the morning, prior to the start of the races, we were testing the equipment. Suzie had been in the bottle. I think Mike may also have imbibed, but to a lesser extent. While we were working on the hydro, Mike glanced up and saw Ken Parks, whom he had helped get started in the sport a few years earlier. Mike walked over and began to visit with Ken.

For some reason, which I never knew, Suzie Hammon was confrontational with Ken. In her state of inebriation, she thought Mike was giving assistance to Ken, so she screamed at Mike to depart from the Parks trailer. Mike ignored Suzie, which further spurred her anger. There then followed a verbal assault, the likes of which had never been heard in the annals of the Oklahoma Boat Racing Association. Needless to say, all eyes in the pits were on the two combatants.

Apparently, words were not sufficient, so Mrs. Hammon began to pick up rocks and hurl them at Mike, who finally took cover behind a large oak tree. The tree was a good shield, but Mike made the mistake of holding on to the tree, with both hands wrapped around it. One of the exceptionally big rocks found its mark, hitting Mike on the fingers of his right hand. He let out a howl and quickly retreated into the woods. It took Suzie a while to calm down, but Mary finally talked her into having a seat and another drink. It was then that Mike emerged with his right hand swollen to the size of a small melon. We later learned that he had several broken fingers, a larger injury than he had ever sustained in his years in the racing wars.

In the early sixties, the modified Mercury deflector engines ruled the roost. The components for these engines were built by a few specialty shops, but the two primary builders were Pep Hubbell in California and Quincy Welding. In our section of the country, almost all the modified components came from Quincy Welding, located at Fifth and State Street in Quincy, Illinois, a community located on the Mississippi River. I was one of the last to field a KG9 Merc in the D class, as most drivers were then using the 55H and later-model powerheads. O. F. Christner, proprietor of Quincy Welding, must have eaten well at that time, because it seemed like we all spent a lot of money buying components for those alky-burning mills. Quincy Welding had a dynamometer, which must have been used twenty-four hours a day because they would continually come up with new pieces and updates to enable you to go faster. Of course, any new component that was introduced had to be tried, so we all participated in the merry-go-round ride.

Not only did Quincy Welding build a lot of innovative racing parts, but the company also fielded one of the top racing teams in the country at that time. They competed several times a year at our Oklahoma races and always provided the toughest of competition. By actually competing, Christner and the members of his team (who were also his employees) could test their theories and new products to stay on top of the heap. All the Quincy drivers were very good, and many national championships came from their big yellow trailer (which hauled six or seven boats and an armada of engines). These drivers included Freddie Goehl, Arlen Crouch, David Christner, Earl Hull, and, of course, Jim Schoch.

The Quincy Welding Team fielded entries in almost every alky-class regatta across the country.

The arrival of the rig, carrying seven boats and a dozen or more engines, would intimidate almost any competitor. This photo was taken in 1960, at which time the boys from Quincy held national championships in five different classes. The Quincy drivers included several standouts, such as Freddie Goehl, Arlen Crouch, David Christner, Earl Hull, and Jim Schoch. (National Outboard Association photo)

In 1962, we decided to make a change, and an Oklahoma City truck salesman, Vance Lee, entered the picture. After some negotiations, Vance purchased Earl's trailer and the Ashburn runabout. I then ordered a brand-new Sid Craft hydroplane which, at that time, was the hottest thing going.

The new boat arrived in a crate the following spring in time to run in the first race of the 1963 season. About a week after its arrival, the new hull was sitting on the bottom part of its crate in the middle of my garage. I was at the office that morning when I received an emergency call from Sandra. She reported there had been a huge gas explosion on the street behind our house, which had started fires that had burned up several houses and was threatening ours. She and our daughter Kathy, who was only four years old at the time, had been instructed by the police to leave the neighborhood, and they had evacuated, leaving everything behind. I immediately left the office and drove home as quickly as possible. Since I knew the family was okay, my only thought was the new boat, and I pictured it in ashes. When I reached Sandra, the first thing I asked was if the new boat had been damaged.

Things turned out okay for us, as the firemen extinguished the fire before our home suffered any damage. Upon reflecting on this situation, Sandra and I became amused, as the first thing our daughter wanted to know was whether her pink party dress had burned up. Sandra wanted to know if our dog was okay, and I wanted to know about the new boat. We all had our priorities, I suppose.

During the next two years, Vance drove the racing rigs, while I continued maintaining the old Merc. Chief was the crew chief and was always there to give us a hand. The competition at that time was tough in the Southwest, especially in the D class, where such drivers as Raymond Owen, Raymond Jeffries, Bill Talley, Bill Weeks, and Leo Fondren were every-week competitors.

One of the last races Vance drove occurred at Lake Dallas, Texas, in 1963. Chief and I had driven down early in my old 1955 four-hole (Roadmaster) Buick. Vance and his wife, Sue, had pulled the rig down the morning of the regatta in his Chevy El Camino pickup. During that morning, while waiting for the Lees, Chief got into the sauce and, by race time, was feeling no pain. Everything was going well until Vance got into a wreck in the D Hydro race and broke his arm. He was toted to the hospital and returned during the final event of the day with a cast on his right arm. During his absence, Chief had continued his one-man party, and by the time Vance returned, I don't think he even recognized him. After the wreck, I was attempting to load up the equipment and dry out the engine when I happened to glance over at Vance's truck. Chief was sitting on the tailgate nodding, when all of a sudden, he fell over, hitting his head against a metal water can in the bed of the truck. That was it; Chief was out for the rest of the trip. At that point, we were facing a grim situation. How were we going to get everything home? We had two vehicles and a trailer to move two hundred miles north on Interstate 35. Chief was incapacitated in the back of the pickup, Vance was hurting and had his right arm in a sling, Vance's wife could not see at night and so was unable to drive, and there was me. About that moment, I felt like taking a gun and shooting Chief. Instead, we left him where he lay in the bed of the pickup; Vance drove the truck home with his left hand, and I drove the second vehicle. What a trip! Believe it or not, we made it home without further incident. I'm still not sure who was in worse shape on Monday, however, Vance or Chief.

During the 1963 season, the foreign motors were beginning to impact racing in the Professional category, and the handwriting was on the wall––the alky deflectors were on the way out! I had to make the decision to either buy one of the foreign mills or go to some other type of racing. At that time, the NOA had its Am Pro Division, in which the four-cylinder Mercs were used. Rules permitted a few modifications and exhaust megaphones, but fuel was limited to pump gas and two-stroke oil. This form of racing was obviously less expensive, and I was already familiar with that type of engine, so I opted to direct my efforts toward Am Pro racing.

To make this transition, I sold my alky burner, bought out Vance's interest in our rig, and purchased a stock 55H Merc from Dub Stone, who had been racing the engine in outlaw OPC events. I then mounted a Quincy exhaust system, made a few minor changes to the engine, and was ready to go racing Am Pro style.

About that time, I ran into Ed Brett, a college student who had been racing a homemade "pumpkin seed" hull in the local OPC outlaw races. Ed ended up driving for me in 1964 and 1965. The Oklahoma Boat Racing Association had no races scheduled for the Am Pro stuff, so we attended events during those two years conducted by the Kansas City Speedboat Association and the St. Louis Outboard Drivers Association, both active Am Pro clubs. During that time, I learned that building an Am Pro (later termed a modified) engine is much different than building an alky burner. Consequently, we lacked the speed to win the big ones. I then "went to school," visiting with anyone I knew who was knowledgeable about these motors. This even included a trip to St. Louis to visit Walter Courtois personally, who was at the top of the heap in the D Runabout Class at that time.

In 1966, the Oklahoma Boat Racing Association, which had been conducting races in Oklahoma and surrounding areas since 1923, had nearly become extinct. During the previous season, only two or three racing events had been held, and prospects were poor that anything would be on tap in 1966. Most of the drivers had quit, and the one-time prolific OBRA had its back against the ropes. Clyde Bayer, a Tulsa marine dealer, and I had discussed our predicament several times, and we both felt that the OBRA should be resurrected. Neither of us was willing to see what we loved go out the window, as had happened in some other states.

Late in the spring of 1966, Clyde and I gathered others who were interested in revitalizing the club and held a meeting at the Howard Johnson restaurant on the Turner Turnpike, halfway between Oklahoma City and Tulsa. I think there were only five or six in attendance, including Leo Voss, Charley Huff, Clyde, myself, and one or two others. I was elected president of the group (since no one else wanted the job). That first year I served as president had to have been the worst year the OBRA had ever experienced. We had only about eight or nine members that year, with no races. What a far cry from ten years earlier, when we were staging ten or eleven shows yearly and had seventy-five members!

The handful of members we did have, however, were determined that we were going to turn things around, and we started working toward the 1967 season. I was reelected president in 1967 (again because I was the only one to take the position, certainly not because of the job I did the previous year). We began contacting various civic groups throughout Oklahoma, and I traveled several hundred miles that year, presenting our program and showing slides to numerous sponsor prospects. Clyde and some of the Tulsa members were also busy attempting to line up sponsors. By the time the smoke all cleared, we had ten races scheduled for the 1967 season at sites all over the state.

Our next hurdle was to make good our commitment to provide an entertaining show for these sponsors. To accomplish this, we had to have boats on the water. We were able to obtain some old mailing lists of drivers formerly belonging to the OBRA and other clubs in nearby states. These were all sent notices of our events, and trophies were offered to the first three place winners in each of the eight classes we decided to include on the program. Added inducements were free jackets, shirts, and other items to all participants at each show. The first few races were sparsely attended by contestants, but we made it a point to give the crowd its money's worth. Everyone cooperated, step-ups were entered when needed, and the programs were successes. The following year (1968) was an even more successful season. We again conducted ten races, and our membership grew substantially. Fortunately, this trend continued for the next several seasons, and the OBRA again became one of the leading outboard-racing organizations in the country.

Oklahoma Boat Racing Association display at the Oklahoma City Boat Show, circa 1965. Displays such as this often appeared in various shows during that time period and were effective in promoting the sport. (photo origin unknown)

In Oklahoma City, the old Overholser Motor Boat Club, which had been going strong since before World War II, was staging outboard races once a month on Lake Overholser, a water reservoir on the west side of the city. Most of the racing featured pleasure boats of various types, and its entry lists included everything from family ski and fishing boats to tunnel hulls and hydroplanes. One class, designated 20 horsepower and under, was dominated by a sprinkling of older hydroplanes and "pumpkin seeds" built from plans found in magazines. From that group of competitors emerged a number of new members who would later play a big part in the reorganization of the Oklahoma Boat Racing Association. These included Rick

Morris, who later became a multinational hydro champion and a cofounder of the American Outboard Federation, Bob Phares, Bob Middaugh, Stan Wakefield, and Ed Brett, all top contenders in later years. This was as enthusiastic a group of racers as I've ever seen. Even during the winter months, several of them would spend their Sunday afternoons tuning their boats on Lake Thunderbird near Norman, Oklahoma. Led by Bob Phares, the group would build bonfires and uncork a bottle of bourbon to keep off the chill. They held some impromptu races that would rival the best national championship events, and these afternoon sessions were termed the "winter circuit." Generally, water conditions were pretty good, in spite of the lower temperatures, but one Sunday in early February, the group was surprised to find the lake partially frozen. Not to be deterred by such an insignificant factor, Phares launched his Neal hydro, busted a path in the ice with his paddle to the unfrozen middle of the lake, and the group continued its winter competition. Unfortunately, the winter circuit was discontinued in the late sixties because of Bob's untimely death, and the remainder of the group stuck to summer racing.

We had a lot of fun with that group from the Overholser Motor Boat Club. Competition among them was nothing short of fierce, particularly among Rick, Stan, and Bob, who all lived in the same neighborhood. Most of their spare time was spent working on their racing rigs, and they were all very guarded as to what they were doing to improve their performance. Stan was particularly serious in his endeavor to gain speed and would lock himself in his garage where he did his motor work and even put sheets over the garage door windows to maintain an air of secrecy. Rick, who was mischievous to say the least, loved to go over to Stan's house and scratch on his garage door during the secret moments, just to let Stan know someone was trying to peek in.

Rick Morris was always a fierce competitor and is a great friend of mine. In his early racing years, Rick campaigned a class-B rig powered by a 20-horsepower Mercury, and he was nicknamed "Mercury" at one time because of his infatuation with that mill and his uncanny ability to extract the most out of it. This nickname left him in later years, however, when he switched to the B-1 Class and eventually became probably the most knowledgeable two-cylinder OMC competitor in the country. His son Richard would later become one of the winningest drivers in that class.

Another OBRA member to impact the rejuvenated organization was a young man by the name of Brian "Butch" Webb, who had moved to Tulsa in the mid-1960s from Illinois. Webb, a pipeline engineer, had started his racing career in Illinois and brought his equipment with him. Butch became one of our most active members and later served as president of the organization for several years.

Webb was probably the most knowledgeable race boat man I've ever met. A real innovator, Butch was the designer and driver of the first pickle-fork hydroplane seen in our area. He was also credited with numerous other ideas he put into practice, some of which are being used in today's hulls. To achieve his innovations, Butch was able to apply the engineering theories and calculations he learned while at Oklahoma State University, along with countless hours of wind-tunnel testing at Tulsa University. As soon as he could come up with a new design or idea, Butch would build a test boat. It seemed like he had a new creation every week, some of which were real eyesores. Some of Butch's ideas didn't pan out, but most of them did. We all looked forward to seeing what he would show up with at the next race. We continually teased him about building those boats over a weekend (which was probably close to being correct).

There are many stories about Butch, a real character (but one of the nicest people you'll ever meet). One story that comes to mind is when Butch built a hydro with water-ski sponsons. The sponsons were attached to the hull so that when the steering wheel was turned, the sponsons were pivoted at angles to permit the boat to turn. The engine was held stationary and locked in a straight-forward position. Webb was very secretive about the new boat and took it to Claremore Lake, about thirty miles north of Tulsa, for a secret test session one weekend. Upon his arrival at the lake, he was somewhat disappointed to find that Clyde Bayer and a whole host of other boat racers were on hand to test their rigs also.

After launching the new secret weapon, Butch fired up his D Merc and roared off down the lake. He quickly ran out of sight, and his engine noise died away. A few minutes later, Butch came walking down the bank, looking dejected. After numerous inquiries, he reluctantly admitted the skis wouldn't turn the hull, and he had run the new creation nearly halfway up the lake's rocky dam.

One of Webb's biggest thrillers was a project he refused to discuss—the infamous "paddle wheeler." He kept this one a dark secret until one evening he and Clyde Bayer were drinking some of Butch's home brew (for which he was well known). Butch was in a melancholy mood and made the big mistake of divulging information concerning the "paddle wheel" experiment. Clyde jumped on this revelation quickly and goaded Butch into showing him an 8-mm film of the experiment. In less than twenty-four hours, everyone in the OBRA (and a few in surrounding states) had heard of this infamous experiment. About a year later, with Clyde's help and Butch's beer, I was also privileged to see this revealing film. To my knowledge, the film has never been shown since, and I still can't believe what I saw.

Butch had mounted an old Merc engine on one of his homemade creations. In the rear of the hull was mounted a huge paddle wheel, which looked like a miniature version of the type of wheel that propelled the old riverboats. The paddle wheel and most of the parts were items that had been removed from various farm equipment. It was all so bizarre that I can't even describe it. Webb was seen in the video proudly showing off the various components of his endeavor, starting the motor and eventually the paddle wheel itself. I can't remember many other details about the experiment, but I do recall that the boat, when under power, experienced very little movement, and it all ended when the farm tools began coming apart. To this day, Butch is very sensitive when you bring up the subject of the infamous "paddle wheeler."

In 1968, Butch built a D runabout that was a flyer, literally. The hull was extremely light in the front end, and was difficult for him to handle. As a cure, Butch drilled a one-inch hole through the sides of the hull at its nose and then mounted a dumbbell with a weight on both sides. The idea behind the dumbbells was that the weights could be changed out to use larger or smaller ones, if the original weights were inadequate.

Butch showed up with the dumbbell boat at a race on Wetumka Lake in central Oklahoma in 1969. As soon as Webb towed the weird-looking craft to the race site, the kidding by the other drivers commenced. Undaunted by the teasing, Butch readied his new D runabout for the race and plotted to get even with the hecklers after he was declared the race winner.

That year, Clyde Bayer and I had been winning most of the D runabout events, and we were expecting one of us to best the field that day. However, Butch had other plans! Clyde and I started the race side by side, slightly in front of the pack, and were running full throttle down the front chute when suddenly Butch poked that dumbbell boat right between us and proceeded to walk away with the race—that is, until he got to the first turn, which was located about a hundred yards in front of the north shoreline. We were shocked to see that Butch didn't make the turn but continued in a straight line toward the bank, on which a number of spectators were perched. The next thing we knew, the spectators were fleeing to the trees behind them just before Butch hit the bank wide open, and the entire rig went completely out of sight into the woods. Fortunately, the trees shielded the spectators from harm. Butch's "boat of the week" was severely damaged, as were some of the trees, whose bark were removed by one side of the dumbbell, but fortunately, Butch was unscathed.

In 1967, a youngster named David Smith, later dubbed "The Kid" due to his youthful appearance, arrived on the scene. David became acquainted with boat racing through Ken Bayer, with whom he had raced quarter midget autos. When I first met David, he was a high school senior who was preparing to attend college on a wrestling scholarship. David had been a two-time state high school champion wrestler; he weighed about 135 pounds and was tough as nails. He had been interested in racing from an early age. In addition to his experience in the quarter midgets, David had also raced go-karts, and his brother Bill had held a world motorcycle drag record.

David possessed a natural talent for racing. He was smart and had triggerlike reflexes and a very competitive spirit. During the next ten years, "the Kid" was to become one of the greatest competitors in our sport and was to bond to our family as almost a member. He was very special to all of us. My kids, Kathy and Phil, thought of him as an older brother, and Sandra and I considered him as our eldest.

The first boat race in which I remember David competing was early in the 1967 season opener at Mohawk Park Lake in Tulsa, Oklahoma. That day, he drove one of Clyde Bayer's rigs, a Dubinski hydroplane powered by a D-modified Merc. Everyone but Bayer was pitted at the east end of the small lake. Bayer's trailer was situated several yards around on the front straight.

Soon after the five-minute gun sounded for the first heat of the D Hydro event, the entire field (or so we thought) pulled onto the course and began the milling process prior to the lineup for the start. Poor starts on a timing clock at the first race of the season is a common occurrence, and this event was no exception. We all were late getting to the line, however, as we rounded turn four and headed to the starting line, we saw a Dubinski hydro pull away from the north bank (about two hundred yards from the starting line) and head toward the clock. David hit the clock perfectly and reached turn one about the same time the rest of us passed the clock. Needless to say, he won that race and made the rest of us look pretty stupid. Today's racing rules require that all entries leave the pits before the last minute prior to the start. However, that rule was not in effect at that time in Oklahoma.

A couple of days later, I received a phone call from David, who now had been bitten hard by the racing bug. He expressed an interest in learning more about the sport and possibly obtaining some equipment. I told him to bring his dad over to the house the next evening, and we would discuss the matter further. They showed up as scheduled, and after a long evening of discussion, we agreed on a partnership. That was the beginning of a ten-year-long relationship I will always cherish.

David "The Kid" Smith, one of the best ever, seen racing a Class D hydroplane on Lake Overholser in Oklahoma City. (Jim Lucas photo)

In December of that year, we bought a J Mar hydroplane from a fellow in Memphis, Tennessee. David, who was home on Christmas break from college, volunteered to pick up the boat on New Year's Eve. He left Oklahoma City early that morning and returned the following day, after traveling through snow most of the way. When he returned, David said the man from whom he picked up the boat must have been in some sort of showbiz, because his hair was so long it grew over his collar. I told him his assumption was correct; the man was Marshall Grant, the bass fiddler of the famous Tennessee Three, Johnny Cash's accompaniment.

That New Year's Eve, I tied one on at a friend's party and suffered the full consequences the following day. When ol' Kid rolled in with the new hydro full of snow, I was almost incapacitated with a headache and all the usual hangover symptoms. We unloaded the boat and laid it on its side without removal of the snow. I told David I would take care of the snow problem after it melted and I felt better, so I went back to bed. Most of the snow did melt that day but, in my misery, I forgot to drain the water. That night, the melted snow froze in the unheated garage. The next morning, I was distressed to learn that the freeze had burst a hole in the right corner of the transom. That's when I swore off booze. (This vow lasted at least a couple of weeks.)

During the next couple of seasons, Kid and I ran a lot of races all over the Southwest. Kid was in college at that time, first at Lamar Junior College in Colorado and then at Idaho State, where he wrestled under a scholarship program. When school was out in May, we immediately hit the old "hot dog and hamburger" circuit until school started again in the fall. During that time, Kid was gaining a lot of valuable experience and honing the driving skills that would later enable him to become one of the top shingle jockeys of the 1970s.

I guess David was a natural athlete. He excelled in everything he tried, but racing was his real sports love. One fall, following a very successful summer boat-racing season, he was approached by the owner of a sprint car who had heard about his boat exploits. He asked Kid if he would like to try his hand at auto racing. The Kid was not one to turn down anything that ran fast, so he quickly agreed to drive the sprinter in a big race in Enid, Oklahoma, in October, which was tabbed the Winter Nationals. The car he drove was not considered one of the better cars in the circuit, as it had not fared well that season with its regular pilot. This was certainly no deterrent for the Kid, who ended up finishing a close second in the "A" Feature race of the Enid event. Needless to say, he was the talk of the track that day, and the other drivers accused the car owner of bringing in a ringer from the USAC ranks. No one believed the car owner when he announced that this was the Kid's first sprint-car race (and it turned out to be his last also).

Another illustration of Kid's natural ability was the day he drove Stan Wakefield's B hydro at Lake McAlester. At that time, Stan was racing an old Neal hydro, considered by most to be obsolete since the Swifts, Sid Crafts, and other hulls had entered the picture. In the late sixties, the B Hydro race was very competitive, with full fields appearing at most regattas. Stan had finished in the pack several times that season, but that year, the boat had not been a frontrunner. This day, Kid and I were sitting on the bank, waiting for our heats to start and watching Stan and the other drivers preparing to go out for the B Hydro event. Kid mentioned something about Stan's rig, and the next thing I knew, he was marching toward Stan. A short conversation between the two ensued, and the next thing I saw was Kid pushing Stan away from his boat and grabbing his life jacket and helmet. Kid then proceeded to push Stan's rig into the water and jump in as the five-minute gun sounded. One pull of the cord, and he was off, with a dumbfounded Stan still standing there. To make a long story short, Kid ended up with wins in both heats of the B Hydro race that day, with everyone wondering how he had done it. He certainly wasn't the fastest, but then Kid could spot you speed and still beat you—that was the Kid! I could write a whole book about this young daredevil but will save more stories for my next book, which will cover the 1970s through the 1990s. Kid was a real racer, a flamboyant character no one who ever knew him well will forget. He was killed, racing in the sport he loved most, at Cross Lake in Shreveport, Louisiana, in 1976.

There are certain events in history that you identify with where you were or what you were doing. One such event was when our astronauts landed on the moon in 1969. Kid and I were en route to a race at Jacksboro, Texas, as we heard all about the landing on the car radio. The moon was full that night, and we felt like we could almost see the guys walking on that celestial body. When we arrived at the race site that evening, we were informed of the shocking news that Raymond Jeffries and his son Duke had been killed that afternoon in the crash of Raymond's experimental airplane. The crash had occurred after Raymond and Duke had tipped their wings in a salutation to those who had arrived early at the race site. The plane had experienced some sort of malfunction and ended up in the side of a building at the end of the lake. The following day, everyone in attendance had difficulty in thinking of anything but the accident, as the building with the burned hole in its wall stared down at us. Raymond had been a great competitor and was popular with everyone. He was one of those people who could make a silk purse out of a sow's ear. I had seen him numerous times walking the banks after a race, picking up used spark plugs and cast-away parts, which found their way on his engines the following week. Jeffries was one of the hardest drivers I ever encountered.

This 1962 photo was snapped at the Guaymas, Mexico Yacht Club awards banquet, which followed a big-money race held there in December of that year. The four winners pictured are, left to right, Raymond Owen, C. B. Norton, Freddie Goehl, and Ted May. The lady in the center is Norton's wife, whose photo was included for "window trimming." All four drivers had been national champions, which indicated the caliber of competition at this international event. (National Outboard Association photo)

During the mid and late 1960s, we raced some in Texas. Most of those events were for the alky burners, so we were outclassed with our AmPro gas jobs. The first time I went down there with a gas burner was to Mineral Wells late one season. A cold front had moved in the day before the race, and the temperature was nippy. A large field of some of the best pro equipment in the Southwest was on hand, and a decent purse was up for grabs. When I saw the caliber of equipment in the pits, I regretted making the trip and considered turning around and heading back north. However, I knew that miracles do occur, and who knows, maybe the weather would chase off part of the field. In assessing my situation, I knew that I had one factor in my favor: the weather, as every engine but mine was propelled by methanol, a high-flashpoint fuel that does not do well in lower temperatures because of hard starting and spark-plug-fouling characteristics.

Sure enough, when the gun sounded for the D Hydro race, my engine was the first to start, and I was already on plane before the rest of the field fired up. It was surprising, however, that almost all the entries, a full field, did get their mills fired and were ready for the start. I knew I had only one chance, so I went for it. I led the field up early by a theatrical presentation in which I crouched down in the cockpit and plainly clamped down on the throttle. Surprisingly enough, the entire lineup followed suit, fearful of being tardy at the start and having to eat a lot of the spray. Just as I arrived a short distance from the starting line, I shut my engine down until I got off plane. By that time, the other drivers realized what had happened and also had to chop their throttles. As the starting flag dropped, I quickly gassed my motor and planed off again, thanks to my gasoline fuel, and I headed off toward the first turn. When entering the turn, I glanced back and found I was enjoying a large lead, with the alky boys experiencing difficulties around the starting line. Some of their engines had completely fouled out, while those still running were sputtering. I ended up winning the race that day, though the alky burners did finally get going and came within about ten feet of running me down at the finish line. That turned out to be a pretty unconventional way to win a race but was one of the most enjoyable ones I ever experienced.

At a race in recent years, I ran into Mel Wilcher, a longtime friend who raced out of the Kansas City area for several years. Mel reminded me of an incident that occurred at a race in the northeastern part of Oklahoma in the late sixties. Mel is a big fellow, about six feet four, who at that time weighed around three hundred pounds. He was competing in a Class D Runabout that day which was running very well. As we approached turn number three on the second lap, Mel hit a wake and plummeted out of the boat right in front of most of the pack. I was close behind and was able to avoid hitting him, but the driver behind me was not so lucky and ran right over Mel, cutting about five pounds off his backside (a helluva way to lose weight, said Mel). The race was red-flagged immediately, and a pickup boat was quickly dispatched to the scene. The pickup boat, however, was occupied only by an aged husband-and-wife team who had been recruited to operate the rescue vessel by the local sponsor. There was no way the senior citizens could get Mel into the boat, so he hung on to the side of the craft while they drove to the shore at a trolling speed.

As soon as Mel reached the shore, the ambulance personnel swung into action. However, the ambulance driver and his female accomplice had spent most of the afternoon listening to tunes on the radio of the ambulance, thus running the vehicle's battery down. Upon checking the injured's back, it was determined that Mel needed to go to the hospital for stitches. As the ambulance was inoperable, Mel himself ended up jump-starting that vehicle with his own pickup so that the ambulance could transport him. What a deal!

A scene at Chickasha Lake, Oklahoma, in 1969. Shown here is Steve Wolfe of Tulsa, Oklahoma, accepting the "checkers" from Dudley Malone. This was the final race of the season, and Steve had just wrapped up enough points to win the Oklahoma State High Point Championship for that season. Steve was a bit wet in this shot from a dunking he had taken from other drivers for his win. Malone was president of the Oklahoma Boat Racing Association that year.

Postrace parties, official or unofficial, were common in the 1950s and '60s. The "official" ones were usually staged by the sponsors or the local racing club, and generally the fare consisted of beer and horse-cock (bologna) sandwiches, plus maybe some watermelon. I don't recall much about most of these outings, but the ones at Lake McAlester, in the southern part of Oklahoma, stand out in my memory. One year, I took Ray Renick, a fellow who worked in my office in Oklahoma City, to one of the annual McAlester events to pit for me. Ray had earlier expressed an interest in the races, as he had never seen one. After that event, I don't think he ever saw another.

The races that day went well, though I don't recall much about them. I do recollect, however, that my tow vehicle, a 1962 Oldsmobile Vista Cruiser station wagon, fondly called the "Greenhouse" because of its similarity to a flower shop's delivery wagon, picked up a noise en route to the race, which turned out to be a valve lifter problem. We received several offers of assistance with the problem from Clyde Bayer, Butch Webb, and Jack Farnam, all of whom resided in Tulsa. Fearful that the Greenhouse wouldn't pull the race trailer as far as Oklahoma City, I agreed to follow the three to Tulsa to attempt a repair. By the time we left the shindig, it was nearly midnight, and we were somewhat numb. We ended up in a caravan on the turnpike to Tulsa with the old Greenhouse running a whole lot faster than it should with the valve problem. The Bayers had a cooler full of beer, and the cans were thrown from car to car as we headed toward Tulsa. While this was going on, I glanced over at Ray, who was white as a sheet but having the time of his life.

When we arrived in Tulsa, we all drove to Butch's residence, and I pulled into his front yard about 2:00 a.m. As soon as I popped the hood, about five drunks started wrenching on the poor ol' Olds, with parts flying everywhere. About that time, Butch emerged from his garage with several bottles of his dad's famous home brew (which was exactly what we didn't need). A few brews later, the mechanics announced their inability to repair the vehicle. Farnam then extracted two spark plugs, announcing that I should be able to get home on the remaining six cylinders. This I was able to do at about forty miles per hour, and Ray and I arrived home just as the sun was rising. We both quickly shaved, showered, and were at the office at eight. You should have heard the stories Ray told at the office that day about his first and last boat race.

In the late sixties, one of my favorite races was the annual Sand Bass Festival event on Lake Texoma. Since this was the same lake on which I started this crazy sport, it was like a homecoming to me each year. Huge crowds were always on hand to see the event, and we always drew good fields of boats from both Texas and Oklahoma, which created a real interstate rivalry. An incident that always stuck out in my mind occurred in 1969, when Bob Viola showed up after about a fifteen-year absence from racing. Most of the drivers who had raced with Bob in the fifties had retired by 1969, so few knew who he was. Bob brought his old Desiiva runabout (which he had raced fifteen years earlier) and a 20-horsepower Mercury. The only prop Bob owned was an old brass wheel.

Most of the other drivers had two or more engines and a multitude of props—all stainless steel. This might have intimidated most guys, but not Bob. He just went to work and spent all morning dialing in his setup with that one fifteen-year-old brass prop. When the checkered flag dropped, it was Bob Viola who was first across the finish line, to the amazement of all of us. Bob was a real competitor, as was his father and, later on, his son Barry.

A lot of drivers went to Vietnam in the sixties. One was Clyde Bayer's son Kenny, who would become very dominant in the sport during the next two decades. Shortly after Kenny arrived home from the war, the Bayers, Kid Smith (who had raced quarter midgets with Kenny earlier), and I decided to team up and race at Corsicana, Texas. Kenny and Kid rode together, pulling the Bayers' rig, while Clyde, a crewman, and I drove our rig. We had purchased a case of beer prior to our departure, and Clyde and I tried fervently to dispose of it on the way to the race the evening before the event. My tow vehicle (an old Ford sedan) had a huge hole in the back floorboard, where a heavy engine had fallen through. I normally kept an aluminum pie pan over the hole to keep out the dust but uncovered it during the trip for a Port-a-Potty while on the road. By sitting in the back seat (with the beer box) Clyde and I never had to have a rest stop and only stopped one time on the trip to gas up the tow vehicles. While we were filling up the tanks, a boy of about twelve years of age stopped on his bicycle to gawk at the boats. Clyde complimented the youngster on his bicycle selection, and the next thing we knew, Clyde was riding on the bike to demonstrate how to jump curbs.

While Clyde was doing his demonstration, a big black limousine drove in with a highway patrolman at the wheel. Clyde then dismounted from the bike and walked over to the limo to inquire who was aboard. The officer told him that "Big Ben Barnes," the lieutenant governor of Texas, was the lone passenger in the back seat. Clyde then walked over, opened the back door, and offered the lieutenant governor his hand. Barnes gladly shook Clyde's hand and, after looking at his big frame, Clyde exclaimed, "You really are a big Ben!" At that we all cracked up and had a good laugh. I think Clyde offered him a beer, but he was turned down. The rest of the trip was pretty uneventful, as I recall. We always seemed to enjoy our trips to the races almost as much as the races themselves.

In 1969, while attending a race in Texas, I ran across Clyde LaFitte from Louisiana, with whom I had become acquainted several years earlier. In the course of our conversation, Clyde mentioned that a friend of his, Ted Lewis, who lived in Shreveport, Louisiana, had done some prop work for him that had turned out well. This sparked my interest, and I obtained Lewis's phone number from him.

When I returned home, I called Ted, introduced myself, and asked if he would consider doing some prop work for me. It turned out that Ted, who had retired from racing several years earlier, was becoming bored with his eight-to-five routine and was very receptive to helping us. This contact was the beginning of a long friendship that existed for many years. Ted eventually wrote what happened to him after that first phone encounter. "So, we went out to the old tin boathouse in my backyard to try to locate some of the tools and propeller pitch blocks necessary for prop design and repair. Now, opening the door of the old boathouse does indeed require a brave man. The technique used is of art, grace, and the agility of a cheetah. You brace one knee into the door to steady it, unlock the big steel padlock, and run like hell! The doors spring open, and an avalanche of junk that rivals a mountain slide springs forth and cascades out into the backyard. The noise upsets the lady next door, and she is instantly at the fence, shaking her umbrella at me. All the neighborhood dogs are barking by now, and I notice that I have just stepped on the tomcat's tail, which has sent him screaming *meow-w-w* and right into the yard with the bulldog!"

Had I not seen that old tin boathouse a couple of years later, I would probably have passed on Ted's account as so much BS, but now I'm almost inclined to believe his writing. Following the opening of that old boathouse, Ted did find his prop tools and subsequently built us some great wheels. Every championship and record-setting propeller used by Kid Smith and me in the 1970s was the result of Ted's expertise and innovations. Over the years, Ted and his wife, Eloise, became two of my most treasured friends. Ted is now deceased, but every once in a while, I run across one of the old two-blade wheels with Ted's name stamped on the hub, and I remember when.

By the end of the 1960s, outboard racing still flourished. It had changed considerably since the postwar years of the late 1940s, and most of the changes were good, but not all. Spectator and entry turnouts had dropped somewhat, but the level of competition was better. Equipment had greatly improved, and speeds had sharply risen. Driver safety was improved with better safety equipment, and the boats were somewhat more stable and safe, in spite of the higher speeds. Boat racing still held its charm over me, and I was enjoying every minute of it.

My original intent was to write about boat racing from my first exposure to it in the years following World War II until the millennium. However, there was so much to write about, it was decided that I would do two writings instead, with the first covering the period of 1945 to 1970 and the second to cover the period of 1970 until the end of the century. Writing is not my forte, but hopefully this has been somewhat entertaining and has offered a view of what boat racing was like to participate in during the years of my coverage.

Boat racing has played a big part in the last seventy years of my life. I thank God that I was able to participate in and enjoy the sport for so many years. In reflecting on my experiences during that time, I realize that God was my protector all along and has enabled me to realize my boyhood dream.

While I've thoroughly enjoyed the great racing moments and the innumerable good times we've had, I mostly value the camaraderie and lasting friendships I've made. I truly believe boat racing people are the greatest!

Made in the USA
Columbia, SC
27 February 2018